About the author

Chuck Spezzano, Ph.D. is a world-renowned
counsellor, trainer, author, lecturer and visionary
leader. He holds a Doctorate in Psychology. From 30
years of counselling experience and 26 years of
psychological research and seminar leadership, Dr
Spezzano and his wife, Lency, created the
breakthrough therapeutic healing model Psychology of
Vision. The impact of this model has brought deep
spiritual, emotional and material change to thousands
of participants from around the world.

11065278

Also by Chuck Spezzano

If It Hurts, It Isn't Love
Wholeheartedness
50 Ways to Let Go and Be Happy
50 Ways to Get Along with Absolutely Anyone
50 Ways to Change Your Mind and Change the World
    (available March 2002)

50 Ways to Find True Love

CHUCK SPEZZANO, Ph.D.

CORONET BOOKS

Hodder & Stoughton

First published in Great Britain in 2001 by Hodder and Stoughton
A division of Hodder Headline

A Coronet Paperback

10 9 8 7 6 5 4 3

A CIP catalogue record for this title is available from the British Library.

ISBN 0 340 79351 1

Typeset by Palimpsest Book Production Limited,
Polmont, Stirlingshire
Printed and bound in Great Britain by Clays Ltd, St Ives plc

Hodder and Stoughton
A division of Hodder Headline
338 Euston Road
London NW1 3BH

This book is dedicated with great thanks
to my wife and perfect mate, Lency

Acknowledgements

Any book is truly a family project. After all, a family gives a writer to the world. I want to express gratitude for the loving support of my wife, Lency, who first edited the book when it was *30 Days To Find Your Perfect Mate*. I would also like to acknowledge our two children, Chris and J'aime, for their love, support and inspiration. I want to thank Kathy Miller-Strobel for her typing and Peggy Chang for her typing, as well as her indefatigable organisation and support. Further thanks to friend and personal editor Sue Allen for clear thinking and support that gives me the heart and energy to write. Acknowledgements to Karen Sullivan whose gifts made this a better book, and to Rowena Webb, general editor, for her vision about this work. I wish to acknowledge *A Course in Miracles* for all that it has taught me, and for the seminal role that it plays in my life. I would further like to acknowledge my clients, workshop participants and past girlfriends who taught me so much. Finally and once again, thank you Lency, my beloved, best friend and sweet helpmate in our journey together. Where would I be without you?

Contents

Preface to the first edition

This book is meant to be an exploration, an adventure. When I first began work as a therapist I was a staff psychologist at a drug rehabilitation centre. I discovered there was one thing more important to the participants in the rehabilitation programme than using drugs – learning vital healing information about themselves, their relationships and their families.

In this book there is a wealth of tried and accurate information that has worked for thousands of people in my therapeutic practice and seminars over the last three decades. This exploration of your mind can save you pain, time and money and, of course, assist you in finding your perfect mate.

To put it simply, the process in this book will work if you want it to. There are a number of exercises presented here that have, in and out of themselves, manifested partners for people.

The lessons work in two major ways: firstly to make room for a partner in your life, and secondly to invite in your perfect mate. The ideas may be strange and unnatural to your way of thinking at first; don't let that concern you, it's part of the process. You will learn and grow as you go along.

Trust your intuition. Whatever 'pops' into your mind is the easiest way besides hypnosis to bypass the well-defended conscious mind. Whether you are aware of it or not, you are using your intuition all the time. Through your intuition you see the world as you believe it to be. At the very least your intuition presents the metaphoric truth, the symbolic patterns of your beliefs. Your mind will present the real truth as you know or think it to be. The mind at deeper levels is almost completely metaphoric, rather than literal; thus your intuition is a powerful and effective tool. When you use your intuition it creates a natural flow of life-giving energy which is helpful to you and others.

The thinking mind and memory are tools, mere house guests, of your ego. They support the prevailing system of personality within you which is why your memory so conveniently supports the story you made of your life, but does not necessarily have anything to do with the ultimate truth (in which there would be no pain present), or even the relative truth (how things really happened objectively). Get to know your intuitive mind; it will help to move you out of dissociative independence and into partnership or inter-dependence.

If answers to some of the questions in this book do not jump into your mind readily, then guess. That will have a much greater degree of accuracy than labouring through your deductive mind to find answers. If you find no answer springing to mind, it may be there is no answer to that question because it was not so relevant to this particular incident. On the other hand, it may mean that you are heavily defended in this area. If it feels as if the question doesn't really matter, it is the former; but if you feel tense or upset, it is probably the latter. Just take some time to dwell meditatively on the subject until the answer unfolds.

This book works on spiritual if not religious principles, because the higher psychological principles are all spiritual. When I refer to 'higher mind' I am using a metaphor to describe an experience available to all of us from within. This term will be new to some people, and may take getting used to, especially by independent people who are used to doing it for themselves! But the 'higher mind' or 'creative mind' is a great time saver, and the most effective part of the mind. It also helps a person graduate into partnership and inter-dependence.

Some people, because of their religious background, are happier using certain words for God, Higher Power, Jesus, Buddha, Mohammed, Holy Spirit, etc. They are all referring to the same internal experience. As you begin to use the higher mind, reactions to religious upbringing may surface as a natural part of the healing process. The term 'higher mind' can easily translate into your religious beliefs because the spiritual psychological principle employed transcends the metaphors of any particular religion. Whatever word you are comfortable with will work best for you, whether you call it 'Holy Spirit', 'Higher Power' or 'creative mind'.

So when I refer to 'higher mind' I am referring to that part of the mind both spiritual and transcendent, whose job it is to take care of problems and conflicts for us. It is that part of us which knows all the answers. It is very powerful and not employed as often as it could be. I have found it a major source of inspiration and information and used it to good effect when faced with major traps or conflicts. It makes any job easier, because it accomplishes through 'being' or grace, rather than through doing.

While using this part of your mind may be unfamiliar at first, it is worth pursuing. I have found that the degree of difficulty in people's lives reflects the extent to which they are trying to do it themselves, rather than letting it be done through them.

It's best to work through this book completing one lesson a day, but if you do not have time to do a lesson every day, or if a lesson is so powerful you'd like to spend a couple of days on it, that's fine. It will not interfere with the process. Trust your instincts about how to use this book. You'll do fine. If you provide the willingness, miracles can happen.

After finding your perfect mate, you will notice these lessons and the principles within them are helpful in many other ways as well. Continue to apply them and they will help you keep your perfect mate.

After reading this book for the first time, you may want to re-explore the principles it contains. There are many ways to do this. One is just open the book and practise the principle on that page. A whole new life may open up for you. There's much to explore. I wish you the very best in your adventure. Happy relationship!

Before You Begin

This book is about many things. It is a primer in the psychology of the subconscious. It is a book about right relationships. But most of all it is a book to help you to allow yourself to find your perfect mate. And if for some reason you are not ready for your perfect mate, the principles will still work for finding your next relationship, or can even be extrapolated to find your next job, or to assist you to take the next important step in your life.

Along with the principles explained in this book and offered to you as tools for your use, comes a certain amount of responsibility. You are asked to remember your integrity, for without it you cannot receive, feel and therefore enjoy what you have manifested. For instance, to keep manifesting relationship after relationship, just so you can try them out, changes what is potentially our greatest source of growth, a relationship, into a game or a trap. Your game can be used to turn money, sex, power, relationships, success, etc., into much less than they are. Your ego likes to collect trophies to build itself up. Gaming is something we do instead of receiving and loving. Games substitute adrenalin and stimulation for happiness. A poor choice, but a common mistake in our society today.

As you begin, please remember the importance

of your growth now and for the rest of your life. Creating your perfect mate is just the beginning. Then it is time to learn of love, intimacy, forgiveness, commitment, communication, letting go and all the other powerful lessons that enable a relationship to grow and unfold. Otherwise you will create perfect mate after perfect mate without being able to be intimate, to love and to enjoy your love.

It is important to recognise whether you are so independent or immature that you pillage the opposite sex. All that 'taking' does is gratify the ego and create an even greater inability to feel, enjoy and receive. It is a trap. You can grow out of this trap if you choose to move forward. We have a great name for this kind of 'taking' in Hawaii. We call it 'cock-a-roaching': surreptitiously taking while pretending you don't need anything. We do this when we haven't yet recovered from our early wounds in our relationships or families.

You don't have to be perfect to have a relationship. If that were so, none of us would have one. But, as you go into a relationship, recognise your need for healing and be willing to let your partner help you. Surely the major purpose of your life is happiness – and this a relationship is able to provide. If you are not happy, then the next most important purpose, healing, is called for. A relationship reveals not only all that needs to be healed, but with a proper attitude and teamwork, it provides the support and means for the healing to take place.

Relationships offer the fastest means of growth –

and the biggest pitfalls. That's what makes relationships the central point of our lives with regard to happiness or distress, or any of the other key aspects of life such as health, money or success.

You don't have to believe in the principles for them to work. If you fully believed in them you wouldn't need this book. But it is important to read and practise these principles as best you can. There are a number of seminal principles and exercises, any of which could manifest your perfect mate. Combined they create openness, willingness, attractiveness and creativity.

These principles and exercises have been developed over a dozen years of marriage counselling and over twenty-two years of work as a therapist. More importantly, I have tested them all personally. Now I offer them to you, as I have to friends and clients, so you can discover, as they have, that the key to freedom and happiness is within you.

Completing these lessons is an investment in your greatness and fullness as a human being. The more you apply them, the more they will expand your consciousness, build your confidence and self-esteem. With this book you are setting out once more on a great adventure: to know yourself and to have the happy life you desire. Good Luck and Good Fortune to you!

Chuck Spezzano
May 1992
Hawaii

Introduction

Opening to True Love – Finding the Beloved

True love means that there is enough love to carry a relationship forward for a lifetime, through learning, healing and growth, and towards an ever-deepening sense of oneness and joy. True love is the realisation that we have a purpose in life, both as individuals and as a couple. This purpose both empowers us and gives us inspiration and fulfilment. It also provides help, inspiration and fulfilment for many others.

Over ten years ago I decided to write this book about finding and keeping true love. I found, as I travelled in Japan, Taiwan, Canada, England, France and Switzerland, that true love seemed to be the main issue with which people were dealing. Sometimes I saw people who would settle for anyone to escape loneliness; others would endure long droughts because of their fear. Some of the people I met had even found a potentially perfect partner, only to have the relationship disintegrate inexplicably.

Fear is at the heart of the reason why someone cannot find their beloved or open themselves to true love with the partner they have. While there are many other symptoms and causes, in the end it all comes down to fear. In this book we shall embark upon a journey to transform this fear. If you are willing and have the courage to venture forth, you will resolve the neediness, independence or sacrifice that keeps you frightened and dissociated. This journey will change you by helping you to let go of the baggage of the past, along with the beliefs and self-concepts that keep you from finding and recognising true love – even when it's right in front of you.

What you need to do is change. Without change, you will be stuck where you are now. Change doesn't mean following a strict set of rules that makes life less fun. It's quite the opposite. Change involves opening doors so that your life – and love – moves in the direction you want it to.

So let's clear the debris from your mind, to allow change to take place. When this occurs, you'll find that your present drought, or the partner with whom you are finding things difficult, will go through an amazing transformation. When you change your mind about your life, your past and yourself, your present situation will change. Maybe you don't have a partner; maybe you have a relationship that isn't working. In either case, that situation will change, and you'll find a type of love that has been missing in your life. Some of you may have chosen partners for the wrong reasons – perhaps as a subconscious way of holding yourself back. The prospect of change may be more frightening for you, but you will find that unsuitable partners will fall away, or that you will be empowered to leave. These are steps forward into the rest of your life.

Many people have partners that are prepared to go the distance, but they don't know how to make changes to take the relationship to a stronger position, to a happier place. Good intentions can only get you so far. This book empowers people to learn about successful relationships, which is, undoubtedly, the most important area of our lives. Successful relationships are our best chance for happiness, our best chance to experience heaven on earth, with the type of love that we all need and long for. Healing relationships can be the fastest way for us to learn and grow, not only in our homelife, but also in every aspect of daily living. If we have true love in our lives, we become a beacon of light and an inspiration to those around us. Successful relationships fill us with confidence and provide us with fulfilment. This in turn spills over into other parts of our lives – our relationships with friends and colleagues, our jobs and, ultimately, our future.

Over a 12-year-period I went from being spectacularly unsuccessful in relationships to becoming an expert on them. During that time I learned hundreds of lessons about successful relationships and some of the most crucial ones are documented in this book.

The issues that affect our relationships are instrumental in deciding so many other features of our lives; including health, abundance, career and creativity. Truly successful relationships lead to a truly successful life. Finding true love and learning the lessons required to nurture and foster this love, can bring the fulfilment and healing all of us need and desire in this life. Not only does this help us to heal and unify our own minds, but we are also able to evolve in our ability to love and to experience joy. True love gives us the motivation to keep moving forward. If we learn the lessons of healing and change, love will grow in our lives. Not only that, but they will also provide the foundations required to heal issues that continue to show themselves in our relationships. When we find our places of weakness and heal them, we are able to transform our relationships. And, as we evolve and heal ourselves more and more, deeper and deeper fractures (points of pain) come to the surface to be healed. The stronger our relationships, the more prepared and confident we are to handle life's challenges.

As you prepare to find true love, *you* will actually become the love that you are looking for. As you let go of the emotional baggage you have been carrying, you will look with new eyes at your present partner, or at the possibility of having a partner. When you let go of your imprisoning past, so will your partner. If you haven't found your partner, you will be freer than ever before to enter into a fulfilling and loving relationship. Finally, as you become ready for your beloved, they will be ready for you.

It is love that gives lasting meaning to our lives. It is love that gives us value and courage and opens our mind to creativity and grace. It heals us and fulfils us, sometimes beyond our wildest dreams. It fills us with joy and happiness. Of course, even couples who have discovered the gift of true love have many steps, stages and issues to go through, because if it is to be successful, a relationship must be a healing, transforming journey.

These days happy couples are rare. Why? Because it takes some work to get past the romance stage and to continue to work together at deeper levels. There are many stages and steps in a relationship, but with each one that you successfully pass, you will heal more of the fear, conflicts, sacrifices, feelings of unworthiness, guilt and old pain. The successful couple sets their sights on each other and naturally moves to join and heal the distance between them as each new problem, challenge or step surfaces, until peace emerges.

The deepest part of our minds is pure love. That's the part of us that is spirit. In this place we are whole and loving. This is covered up by many conflicts and self-concepts, but it is available to all of us, if we are able to go on to complete our adventure in healing and self-discovery. This book is the beginning of a lifelong adventure in learning and love.

While the idea of true love is attractive to some folks, it is quite off-putting for those who consider themselves beyond the starry-eyed phase, or those who have become veterans of foreign and domestic wars in the relationship arena. Many have become cynical about love through their own misadventures and fear. True love is not some fantasy idea of romance and 'happily ever after'. True love is just the beginning. Only child-rearing requires more in terms of love, nurturing and communication. Finding true love will take willingness, openness, learning, growth, love, surrender, forgiveness, understanding, acceptance, giving, receiving, letting go, joining, humour, healing, the desire for truth and, above all, commitment. True love is both a lesson to be learned and a gift to be embraced. Over the years I have met people who obviously had this gift for love and these same people were often the ones most paralysed by relationship or heartbreak conspiracies. I have met people who were frightened of love and intimacy, in spite of being beautiful and gifted. You may be worried that you do not have the gift for love, but it exists in all of us, at our most central core. It's something you can learn and grow into. It's something you can find within yourself.

True love is one of the few gifts continuously generating joy and willingness. This is a book that can help you have what you so richly deserve. May this book bless and empower you.

Chuck Spezzano, PhD
25 August 2000

Beloved

I came looking all my life to find you.
You brought me to my senses.
Before you, I was a foolish man, a wild man, a
  wounded man.
I was untamed, trusting no one with this runaway
  heart.

Now I am a student in the school of your love
Sitting at your feet, picnicking on the bridge between
  us.
You brought me so generously to love, to myself,
  to the Friend
You patiently waited for my heart to breathe again.

Before you, I was frightened to enter the banquet
  hall.
I was like a man starving at the feast
Now I wait for every exquisite course of you.
I can look in your eyes and see my own
I can swim in the eternity of love that opens between
  us
When the Beloved gazes back at me with such
  longing.

You know and He knows that I have been lost
  without you both.
I was a wild man, a foolish man, a desert man

Thinking I was alone and having to do it myself
Priding and pitting myself against the desert in me
  – foolishly thinking it could never kill me.

Finally your oasis drew near
My soul pleaded with me for honesty
I came home to find what had been missing,
To find what I pretended I didn't need.

So you tamed this foolish man with tenderness
  and beauty
You taught me the sweet rewards of the courage
  to love
With you I walk out of the hells of my own making
Children laugh, gardens beckon
With you I walk the path to paradise.

WAY 1   Your Mind is a Beautiful Thing

Your mind is a beautiful thing because it has limit-less potential. Usually our lives are so bound by limits that at times we feel overwhelmed by all we seem to be up against. It is our nature to want to transcend our limits. The Sufi mystic, Rumi, said we must take 70,000 steps of darkness into light to reach heaven. Whether that number is literally accurate or not, it contains a metaphoric truth about what it takes to reach an enlightened consciousness.

Our mind has the ability to heal, to realise truth, to manifest desires, to transcend time, to solve difficult life problems and much, much more. Most people are afraid of the power of the mind and remain trapped in situations as if attempting to prove they are powerless. But, because I have worked with many thousands of victims, I know the mind's ability to find solutions in the most seemingly impossible situations. When people really are willing to find the way out of a situation, the answer, or at least the doorway to the answer, appears.

Scientists tell us we use 4 per cent of the mind's potential. In the 1970s people thought we prob-ably used about 12 per cent, but in the last two decades we have reached a better understanding of the power of the mind. I call this 4 per cent the 'conscious mind'.

The part of your mind that supplies most of the answers is the higher mind. This is the best name for the part of our mind that has all the answers. Your whole life will get easier when you begin to work with that part of your mind, because its specific job is to solve your problems and it does so with such speed that it makes it seem as if our conscious mind is part of the problem, rather than, as you might think, part of the solution.

Exercise

Every day, write down your answers or thoughts provoked by the exercises. You may also like to keep a daily diary of your progress towards your perfect mate. Choose a problem in your life and write it down as specifically and concretely as you possibly can. Experience any feelings associated with it. Imagine you are willing and have the courage to find the solution. Imagine turning this entire problem over to your higher mind. There are only two minds: your higher mind and your personality mind. The personality mind is totally devoted to making up a story about you and your specialness. You are making yourself special when you feel a lack of self-worth. The higher mind that knows your real value only wants to give you the grace to heal all your problems. Be willing to do anything you are inspired to do to shift the problem. Whenever you think of the past, just know it is being handled for you. Getting the answer is easy. Not getting the answer is difficult. Whether you are looking for a partner or have one, learning to use your creative or 'higher mind' can be both an important and easy lesson. It will always work to show us the answer unless there are ego attachments or self-concepts that we refuse to release.

If you do not have a partner yet, ask your higher mind to bring true love to you, or to show you very clearly what is preventing you from finding it. Once you have been shown what is holding you back, you can ask your higher mind to release you from the attachments to things that you thought would make you happy.

If you have a partner, ask your higher mind to take you to the next step. Or, if you are feeling courageous, ask to be brought to the whole next stage of intimacy and success. If you are held back by a certain problem, be aware that there is fear at the root of the issue. Do not ask for the problem or symptom to disappear. Instead, ask that the fear generating the problem disappears. In this way you will naturally move on to the next step or stage in your journey to true love. How do you do it? Use your higher mind simply to dissolve or remove the illusion of fear.

I have found that using the higher mind can be of great help in problem-solving, finding answers, or in life in general. Just discovering and using this part of your mind can save a lot of time and effort. In my experience, the more we partner with our higher minds, the more we open our emotions and needs so that they can be healed. We open to partnership with those around us, which opens us spiritually, emotionally, and romantically to whole new levels of relationship. It also encourages our *ability to receive which is an important part of a loving relationship.*

Even if the concept or experience of a higher mind is totally unfamiliar, begin to experiment. What you discover may prove to be of the highest value to you.

WAY 2 Feel the Joy

Most people think that first you find a partner and then you feel joyful. Actually, it works the other way round. Your partner comes along because a level of energy and joy, which is hugely attractive, begins to well up inside you and attracts your perfect mate. The more you feel joy the more beautiful you become. Just as when spring arrives and all the flowers begin to bloom, so naturally the bees appear. So much would just come to us if we chose joy first and let that be a part of our lives. If you are joyful, you have already achieved the purpose of a relationship, and a partner appearing or your present partner falling in love with you all over again is a natural result.

Joy is a choice we can make all the time instead of choosing our stories. It is a choice for love instead of fear. At a subconscious level, every problem we have has the purpose of causing something to happen that will bring us joy. But some choices we make are grave mistakes bringing us many things other than happiness.

If you think it is your partner's job to make you happy, you are placing inordinate pressure on the other person. Your partner can never succeed at *making* you happy because of the nature of expectations and demands. Make no demands, have no expectations. Instead, give all you can and love all you can, especially in those areas where you want things from your partner because that will create joy and receiving in your relationship. Your joy is the best gift you can give your partner. It is irresistible.

Exercise

Today, if you experience anything other than joy, say to yourself: 'I could be feeling joy instead of this.'

At the beginning of the day, and at every hour, choose joy. If you find yourself caught in something you don't like admit you don't want it, recognise it is not ultimate truth because it is not joy, let go of any hidden payoffs that you gain from the bad feelings, turn it over to your higher mind and once again choose joy.

This is the best gift you can give to your partners, your parents, your children, the world and God. Anything else is really just a form of revenge.

I am choosing to have joy in every moment of my life!

WAY 3 The Importance of Value

Value gives importance. Thus self-value gives you your experience of importance. Your life, your experience, and what the world deals out to you, all reflect your hidden feelings about your own value.

The bad news is most people value themselves very little. The amount of guilt and unworthiness people experience leads them into sacrifice (which is the kind of giving that blocks receiving), to work hard rather than intelligently, and to live out roles (more of the same kind of giving which allows no receiving and never lets the giver collect a reward). Roles lead to 'burn-out' and trying to compensate for a lack of self-value. That same lack of self-value drives people into doing and doing and doing. It does not allow peace, joy and abundance.

The good news is guilt and unworthiness are not the truth. Guilt is simply a mistake you beat yourself up for. Guilt keeps you stuck. It locks the mistake in place, preventing you from learning the lesson that can be naturally learned from it. But all guilt can be resolved. Across many years of plumbing the depths of the mind, I have found three significant layers of guilt that lead to feelings of valuelessness, self-punishment and grievances toward others.

The first layer of guilt arises when we feel we have done something wrong or, rather, when we

feel we did not do right. The first layer sets up
self-attack and self-punishment, while the second
layer is much deeper and generates most of our
victim and 'scarcity' patterns (see page 223). This
second layer is also responsible for a general lack
of success in every area, and it stems from the guilt
we feel when we are unable to help or to save our
family and its members. We may feel grievances,
judgements and wounds, but these feelings just
serve to hide our sense of guilt and valuelessness.
The third level of guilt is the fracture or separation
we experience from our inner selves and God. All
of this guilt generates unworthiness and blocks our
ability to receive.

Guilt is a psychological trick of the ego that keeps
us from learning the lesson, correcting the mistake
and moving forward to a new level of love and
abundance. Guilt actually forms part of our ego,
which uses this emotion to hide fear and to ensure
its own continuity. To regain our value, it is crucial
that we see guilt for what it is – a psychological form
of control – and to embrace our true value.

To free ourselves from guilt, we must forgive
others. Resentment, bitterness and anger simply
represent hidden guilt that we have projected on
to others. Forgiveness frees us all. The next step
is to forgive ourselves. This naturally adds to our
feelings of self-worth.

It is your sense of self-value which ultimately
allows you to attract a mate of similar value. Feelings
of self-value also create the kind of experience you
have with that mate. If you want a perfect mate, you

must learn to let yourself be a perfect mate.

Exercise

Today, become aware of what you think of yourself by how you act and by how the world acts towards you.
How I think of myself:

_____

_____

_____

Notice when you are feeling unhappy and when you are compensating for feeling unhappy by sacrifice, by keeping busy, or by seeking mindless pleasure. These activities just hide places of valuelessness.
I feel unhappy when:

_____

_____

_____

When you catch yourself in a situation which makes you aware of your lack of self-value, make a new decision about yourself.
The new decisions I have made:

_____

_____

_____

Today, forgive yourself for everything you felt you did (or did not do) that made you feel guilty. For anything you cannot forgive yourself, ask yourself this question: What purpose does not forgiving myself serve?

Realise that for every instance where you feel you failed your family, you have the gift that will free both of you from its problems, past and present. You can move through a level of hidden valuelessness and guilt once you reclaim this gift, which has been there inside you all the time. Remember that it may be buried under pain, grievances and guilt for having failed them, but it is there nevertheless.

As you remember painful incidents or problems that family members have or had, ask yourself what healing gift would transform them? This is the healing gift inside you. As you imagine yourself giving this gift to your family or that relative, to past or present love partners, you will find that they – and the past or present situation – seem to improve. If they or the situation has not fully improved after giving the gift, then there is another gift inside you yet to be given. Continue in this fashion until that past or present situation feels entirely transformed.

Forgive God. This may seem ludicrous, but under every grievance toward someone else, we have been blaming God. Forgiving God frees your higher mind and opens you to be a channel of grace for the world.

Ask your higher mind: 'What is my value?' Hear and feel the words that come to you. Take these words and their feelings deep inside yourself. If you have a bad feeling about yourself or you carry a judgement against someone else that makes you feel badly, then use this exercise to move past it.

A simple way to get past valuelessness is to give something. When you give something to someone, you give them value. When you give yourself to someone, you are giving them great value. The value you choose to accord others by giving to them, you accord to yourself. True giving moves people past deadness in life and relationships and lets change begin again.

WAY 4   The Purpose of Life

The purpose of life is happiness. Simple enough, but most of us take wrong turns on the Highway to Happiness. When we are not happy, then healing becomes our primary purpose. The purpose of a relationship is firstly to be happy and secondly, to heal. True love relationships are meant to last our whole life long as a loving, learning and growing partnership. Healing in relationships comes from love, communication, forgiveness, joining, bridging the differences, letting go, trust, integration, commitment and many other healing principles.

When you are living your purpose, you experience fulfilment. Each of us has a personal purpose, which only we can fulfil. Each relationship has its own purpose, some are simply to learn a certain lesson or heal a certain problem. You can tell the level that you are living your purpose in your relationship by how much fulfilment you feel as a result of the relationship.

Most of the problems in our lives and in our relationships arise from our fear of the greatness of our purpose, and the greatness of the love that occurs both personally and in our relationship. If we live our purpose, we not only help ourselves but we help those around us. Most chronic problems that we experience individually and in our relationships are a conspiracy set up by us out of fear of embracing intimacy, success and purpose. Fully embracing our purpose allows most of our problems to fall away except those necessary for learning about our purpose.

Relationships provide the motivation and the fuel for completing our personal purpose – the means for us to reach happiness. They give us the support to heal ourselves as we progress through life. They expose our wounds from the past in order to make our continued growth possible. The past is relived in present relationship patterns, giving us the opportunity for healing. Heartbreak in a relationship has its roots in the past and is a reliving of a past heartbreak, therefore as the past heartbreak is healed, the present one heals too.

Exercise

Your higher mind will help you live your purpose and realise your happiness. It has a plan for your happiness, which will succeed. Be willing to let go of your plan for happiness. Look at how much of your plan has actually worked. Your subconscious intentions have clearly created other results than those your conscious mind intended. Here you have evidence of a split mind.

Your higher mind is a place of wholeness without ambivalence, and it unequivocally wants your happiness. Examine your life and your love relationship. They have the purpose of happiness. This means moving beyond the ego, its needs and specialness, into new areas of joining and love, which creates joy and happiness. Now begin to think about what your personal purpose is and what your relationship purpose is. It is usually something that both frightens and thrills you, something so great it seems impossible to accomplish. Left to your own devices, it might be impossible, but love and grace make anything possible.

Let go of your plan for happiness and let your higher mind be in charge. Be willing to do anything you are inspired to do, but let your conscious mind be at rest. As you develop a relationship with your higher mind, you will become naturally more inter-dependent with those around you, including the person who will become your perfect mate. Inter-dependence is a natural prerequisite to finding the perfect mate and keeping him or her. Remember your desire for the right relationship is a natural part of your purpose in life. You deserve your perfect mate and you deserve partnership.

What I really want is:

_____

_____

What I have is:

_____

_____

Now imagine what you really want in your life around your relationship and its purpose is melting together with what you have. When it melts together, if there is anything that comes up afterwards that feels or looks negative, integrate that and your higher mind into what has already been melted together. Continue this until there is peace, expectancy and joy. If you are working on a chronic problem you will usually come to a place that contains a major negative feeling. Simply melt it, your higher mind and what was integrated before, into a new level. Soon you will feel the peace again.

I choose to have what I truly deserve, the perfect partner and the best in life.

WAY 5 You Have What You Want

With this lesson we begin our first major foray into the subconscious mind. What you have in your life is exactly what you want because that is what you have made and brought to yourself. The way to have something different is by changing your mind because that allows you to change your world.

One of the biggest traps we face in life is playing the role of victim, thinking we don't want what we have. Once you begin to realise you are making the choices, albeit in split seconds and then repressing them, you can start choices more consciously and have a much better chance of getting what you really want. I have saved myself from death, a car accident, numerous colds and flu, simply because I became aware of that split-second decision which we bury immediately to avoid taking responsibility. Through using this principle I've helped people from all walks of life free themselves from thousands of painful situations.

The first step is to look at the principle 'you have what you want', in the light of your own life. Consciously nobody wants pain, yet only this morning a woman told me the only time she was at peace was after she hurt herself. Hurting herself was her way of attempting to pay off guilt. But self-inflicted punishment does not resolve or even lessen guilt. It

is merely a stopgap measure, which doesn't work.
When we hurt ourselves, we feel bad, which is
just another name for guilt. So when we punish
ourselves, we end up compounding our guilt.

There are several key dynamics which create situations we appear not to want: fear, seeking attention (an
attempt to get love or win back a relationship), getting
our needs met (trying to be special or different),
revenge, holding on to a past relationship, attacking
someone while pretending to be innocent, trying to
hold the family together, attempting to control someone to get them to sacrifice themselves for you, as an
excuse, as an attempt to defeat someone, by trying
to be right or to prove something, by trying to get
something, by trying to control ourselves and others,
and many more. One of the most common attitudes
I find in single people who are avidly looking for a
relationship (but failing to find one) is fear of losing
their independence or freedom. They are unaware that
paradoxically it is only through commitment that we
experience true freedom.

As you begin to explore experiences in your life,
especially why you don't have your perfect mate,
many feelings may come up: anger, defensiveness,
denial, guilt, hurt, doubt, shame, disbelief, and
sadness. Just experience them and notice you are
experiencing them. No negative feeling is ultimately
accurate. This principle is the basis of all healing and
is the reason why all painful feelings and situations
can be transformed.

Remember, the purpose of examining the principle
'you have what you really want' is to free you

from the invariable prisons, buried pain and the accompanying guilt which have been with you all along, just waiting for a chance to show themselves. As you experience negative emotions, try repeating the mantra, 'this feeling is not the truth.' This type of exploration is the beginning of a journey of empowerment. Many people spontaneously recognise and free themselves of blocks just by applying this principle to their lives. Many answers just pop into their minds intuitively.

Exercise

OK, you want your perfect mate. Yet something has been stopping you. This next exercise is a gem for helping the mind discover that blocking hidden agenda.

Pretend for a moment you really don't want a partner! Now, we know you do, but for the purpose of this exercise pretend you don't. As soon as you can imagine that, move on to the next step. Write down all the reasons which come into your mind why you don't want a partner.

I don't want a partner because:

_____

_____

Consider what you have written as your subconscious agenda. Choose once again what it is you really want in the light of this new information.

What I really want is:

_____

_____

_____

Answer the following questions to help you accept your accountability for what you have in your life at present. You will begin exploring your subconscious mind and the hidden 'benefits' you secretly derive from situations you consciously don't want. These questions can be used to explore other areas of your life, but today concentrate on the question of the absence of a partner:

What does this allow me to do? Or, putting it another way, what does not having a mate, or not taking the next step with my present partner allow me to do?

_____

_____

What is it I don't have to do as a result of not having a partner, or not taking the next step with my present partner?

_____

_____

What is my purpose in not having a partner, or not taking the next step with my present partner?

_____

_____

How does this make me special?

_____

_____

What am I afraid of?

_____

What sacrifice am I afraid of?

_____

What guilt am I paying off?

_____

Why don't I feel I deserve a partner?

_____

Who would I be untrue to, if I got my perfect mate?

_____

Who am I getting revenge on by not succeeding in this?

_____

What am I trying to get by not having a partner or by not taking the next step with my partner?

_____

What am I afraid I would lose if I had a partner or took the next step with my partner?

_____

Who am I trying to control by not having a partner or not taking the next step with my partner?

_____

_____

Who am I trying to defeat by not having a partner or not moving forward with my partner?

_____

_____

What am I trying to prove by not having a partner or not moving forward with my present partner?

_____

_____

What am I getting to be right about?

_____

_____

How does this situation defeat my purpose? What frightens me about my individual and relationship purpose?

_____

_____

What change or success don't I feel adequate enough to deal with?

_____

_____

What am I attacking myself and God for by having this situation be the way it is?

_____

_____

Prioritise the questions that seem the most powerful to you. The answer to any one of these questions can, depending on its content, stop you from having your perfect mate or from taking the next step with your present partner. If you don't like the answers that have come up, as they are holding you back from having a partner, take a few moments to make some new choices.

I am turning over to my higher mind the following areas where I feel helpless and unable to change:

_____

_____

WAY 6 Saying Yes to Life

To get what you want you will have to change. If you stay as you are, you will go on receiving what you have now. Change is one of the greatest blessings on earth, yet it is fear of change, or fear of the unknown, which most commonly blocks us. But to grow and reach our higher goals we must change. I've worked with many people who would rather keep the devil they know than reach for the angel they don't. Years of studying the dynamics of relationship problems have taught me that fear, fear of the next step to be precise, is at the core of all problems. Since most of your problems have the purpose of delaying your next step in order to protect you from your fear, when you take the next step it resolves the problem you are facing now. Many people have said to me: 'Tell me what my next step is and I'll take it.' But, even when they know what it is, most people avoid taking their next step because of fear.

So, we have to trust and take the next step forward, not knowing what it is, but reminding ourselves it will be better, just like every other step forward we have ever taken. Of course, taking the 'next step' isn't literally taking a step. It is being open to change, saying 'yes' to life, committing to moving forward. When this happens, life actually seems to change around us. One powerful way to look at life is to regard our major problems as fear of taking the next developmental step in life. That will help us to focus on the real issue rather than its numerous and confusing symptoms.

One of these major developmental steps, a crucial cornerstone step, is immediately before you now: the step of having your true partner or going to a new level with your present partner. When you say 'yes' and are willing to take this step, you will open yourself up to new life and new horizons.

Exercise

Sit quietly and close your eyes.

Imagine the next step awaits you and you can say 'yes' to it, 'yes' to change. You don't have to figure out what it is, or how to do it. All you have to do is want it, be willing for it to happen, knowing it will be better and further forward than where you are now. Take one step at a time. You can handle each step, especially with the help of your higher mind. Right now it's important to concentrate solely on what is before you.

Say YES to the next step. Say 'yes' to your perfect mate.

I am willing to take the next step towards finding my perfect mate.

I am willing to take the next step with my partner.

It only takes an instant of sincerely choosing to have this happen.

WAY 7 Opening the Door

Once, years ago, I broke up with a girlfriend. Our relationship had begun as a friendship and became something more. I had always thought we would retain that friendship no matter what happened. But when we did break up I felt that everything was lost. I can remember how angry I was at first, but I soon got over it. I began looking around for eligible dating partners. It seemed as if all the eligible women had moved out of the city. I was a young doctor, athletic, romantic, attractive enough. Yet there were no eligible women around. I couldn't understand it.

Four and a half months went by, which was a record for me in not finding and dating someone I found attractive. At that time I became a support staff member at a three-and-a-half-day workshop. On the very last day of the workshop, while thinking of my lack of dating partners, I had an intuitive flash that I had slammed the relationship door at the end of the last one. So I decided to open the door and within the hour I had met someone I was attracted to who let me know that she was very available. Within a week I met two more very eligible dating partners and proceeded to make up for lost time. This taught me a very important principle: relationships wait on invitation and not on time; your perfect mate awaits your invitation, not just a special time or place.

In the same way, the point at which your present relationship is stuck reveals a closed door. This door may have been closed in childhood, but typically it will have been closed at the end of a previous relationship. Whatever your relationship situation, it is time to open the door to a whole new level.

Exercise

If you are not in a serious relationship, or haven't been in one for a while, take a look to see if you have slammed the door of relationships on your perfect mate – maybe after your last relationship, or even as a child with your parents.

Ask yourself: 'Am I ready for my perfect mate, or do I want more time to learn and build up confidence with light relationships along the way?' It is important to accept wherever you are, as this will, paradoxically, help you to unfold and advance. If you are in a relationship, ask yourself if you are ready for the next level of success.

Consider whether you have ever opened the door to your perfect mate, or for your present partner to become your perfect mate.

Imagine that you can feel or see the door inside you which you closed. See yourself walking to that door and doing whatever it takes to open it. Remember this is your door: it will be any way you picture it. And as you open it you will experience a new openness that can last.

Just open your door.

Relax – enjoy yourself and feel the expectancy.

WAY 8 The Power of Forgiveness

Many people prevent their perfect mate finding them because they are holding on to major grievances against their parents or old lovers. Such grievances lock you in the past. The anger or withdrawal that occurred then stops you from realising your present possibilities. Forgiveness frees us from the past.

Sometimes sacrifice is confused with forgiveness. People become afraid to forgive because they think if they do forgive, what they don't like will continue to happen to them. That is sacrifice, not forgiveness. Forgiveness releases you from the situation you don't want so that both the forgiver and the forgiven are freed. Forgiveness is the solvent that releases the superglue of grievances and guilt.

Judgement and grievance always hide subconscious guilt. Forgiveness releases the guilt, conscious or subconscious, which is part of every problem. Grievances and guilt are distracting and can stop personal growth. Transform them through forgiveness and thus free yourself from unpleasant behaviour patterns that block your ability both to attract and to receive.

Exercise

Today, allow to come to mind any problems or griev-ances, from the past or present, which may be holding you back from your perfect relationship or your present partner. Under every problem or grievance is hidden guilt. Allow the person, or persons, you need to forgive to come into your mind. Be willing to free yourself and the person you are forgiving from the destructive power of that hidden guilt. Forgiveness releases us from that which we blame on others and ourselves. There are numerous forgiveness exercises. Here are two excellent ones.

Write down who, and what it is, you have a grievance about. Ask yourself: 'Would I blame myself for this?' If you can answer 'no' to this question then both you and the person you were judging are released.

We can be very poor at forgiveness because, as human beings, we always want to be right. Being right always hides guilt and destroys happiness. The easiest form of forgiveness is to turn the grievance over to your higher mind to handle for you. Let your higher mind accomplish the forgiveness.

WAY 9   Feeling Your Feelings!

Your feelings add richness and dimension to your life and make you more attractive. You don't have to feel your feelings to manifest your perfect mate, but you do if you want to enjoy a long and happy relationship. Your ability to feel your feelings correlates with your ability to be a partner and to commit yourself to a relationship. But I want you to make a distinction between feeling your feelings and the amount of feeling you display. Some people avoid their true feelings by expressing many kinds of other feelings. This can become a form of hysteria. Negative emotions are sometimes used as blackmail or revenge, or as a form of immaturity, depending on the way they are expressed. But just as an over-emphasis on your feelings or the expression of negative feeling can be counter-productive to good relationships and a form of avoidance, so can dissociation from your feelings.

A successful relationship is possible when we move from dependence and independence with others into inter-dependence. As we get in touch with our feelings we become more able to relate. Part of the movement from independence towards inter-dependence is being able to re-associate ourselves with our feelings and our body. And as we get in touch with our negative feelings and release them, our ability to receive and experience increases. Fully experiencing your feelings and expressing them does not mean indulging in them, or using them to attack or emotionally blackmail someone to try to see that your needs are met. Experiencing your feelings is not an excuse to act them out or to be immature. It presents a chance to become more mature and compassionate towards yourself as well as towards others.

It takes courage for someone to move towards inter-dependence because of the amount of suppressed and repressed emotion we discover that we have to move through on the way. Feeling our feelings lessens self-denial, makes our subconscious mind more conscious, and increases both our honesty and integrity. All of which makes us more attractive.

Exercise

One of the simplest forms of healing is to experience your negative feelings or emotions until they disappear. You can do this whenever you are not feeling great.

All you do is allow yourself to feel the feelings as intensely as possible, even exaggerate them. Observe everything about your feelings, explore the minute and distinct sensation of each emotion. You will find that as you do they will begin to shift. Once started, don't stop until you are feeling great. Feelings, even the most chronic ones, have an end. Even if you hit a gusher of repressed emotion, it is unlikely to last more than a few days. But you will be happier, feel healthier and be more able to receive afterwards. Experiencing your negative emotions until they are gone heals and moves you forward in your life.

If in this exercise you hit a feeling of deadness or emptiness, or nothingness, or you just feel blocked and have hard-to-identify non-feelings, that's fine. Strangely enough, they are just different kinds of feelings. Just feel them until they transform and you can move to the next level. Most of us are afraid of negative emotions. But this simple tool, truly feeling your feelings, will give you an attractive courage and maturity. Practise feeling your feelings all day today. You can do that and do everything else.

Today, experiment and follow at least one negative feeling all the way through to a good feeling.

What I have learned about my feelings:

_____

_____

The positive feelings I expressed today were when:

_____

_____

The Truth Will Set You Free!

Many people are frightened of relationships because they are afraid of sacrifice. They fear they will become a love-slave in the way they did in the past, and that is enough to keep anybody independent. This is another stage in relationships that we have to face. Too many times relationships die here. Even true love can flounder if you do not know the way. Yet the extent of your independence is a reflection of the amount of sacrifice and dependency you still need to heal. In a successful relationship all three of these roles, sacrifice, dependency and independence are healed. If you want to grow as a person, you will have to face these cornerstone roles sooner or later.

These roles begin in childhood with a trauma, some kind of emotional loss, which was never resolved or mourned. The role becomes a pattern that typically repeats itself in your life. All three roles – sacrifice, dependency and independence – are surreptitious forms of taking combined with an inability to receive. If we fail to resolve these counter-productive roles, deadness in our relationships is the inevitable result.

Not knowing how to handle deadness and boredom keeps many people out of committed relationships, or relationships altogether. Yet for a successful relationship and life, they have to be handled. You have to learn these lessons sometime. Through many years of studying deadness in relationships, I have discovered a number of ways of healing, transcending or resolving the deadness. The bottom line is deadness can be healed because it never is the real truth. It is just something to heal. Deadness is a cocoon we have woven and wrapped around ourselves to keep out emotional pain. It is a form of control to prevent things or people coming to mean so much to us that we can be hurt – again. Deadness lets others know we are 'special' and subtly, or not so subtly, is a form of attack.

Deadness comes out of our roles, rules and duties – doing the right thing for the wrong reasons. It is a place of blindness and deafness to the world and relationships around us. In the deadness we have gained so much control, become so sure we have the answers, that we limit the input from the outside world to almost nothing. Roles are a failure to make contact while looking like you are in contact; living life from rules, but as good as those rules may seem, they begin to get old. Life cannot be lived from rules; they destroy your ability for intimacy and authenticity.

Fusion creates deadness. Fusion is not knowing the boundaries between you and others. When they feel pain you suffer. Fusion, or over-closeness, automatically suggests sacrifice that falsifies giving and disallows receiving. We have a great deal of fusion that needs healing in our relationships. As children, there was often one parent with whom we didn't get on so well while with the other we were extremely close and in 'fusion'. This is the parent with whom we have deeply hidden issues because our feelings are so powerful that we cannot communicate. Fusion leads through sacrifice to 'burn-out', to feelings of repulsion, or even revulsion.

Two well-hidden causes of deadness are competition and 'fear of the next step'. If you believe you are the best, it creates a subtle (or not so subtle) atmosphere in your relationships that communicates to others that there is no equality and therefore no risk of intimacy. Some people win the competition game so strongly they have no space for a partner even though they are seeking one. Once you are the best, there is no room for anyone else.

How much someone means to you generates both your feelings and their value to you, making you feel alive and at the same time aware of the risk of loss. It is the possibility of our partners becoming too important, meaning too much that breeds aliveness in a relationship but when we are afraid of feeling that intensely we seek to control and become afraid to take the next step with our partners. Fear of the next step leads to a sameness that is deadening. One of the easiest ways to move through feelings of deadness is just to be more willing to move forward in your life. It is that willingness which creates change, because life changes as you become ready for it to change.

Dissociation from your feelings is the last aspect I shall mention here, which creates the experience of deadness. Severe deadness in a relationship, or in yourself, speaks of extreme feelings that have been repressed. Some feelings are so painful that we forget them, then forget that we have forgotten them. These feelings are so painful that we would feel like dying were we to discover them. But they are waiting to be healed and your willingness alone can take you into the old storehouse of feelings.

There is a simple way to heal feelings that hurt that bad – service. Whenever you feel so bad that you want to die, if you give or choose to be in service to another, those feelings become a birth, instead of a death, situation. Much more could be said about how to heal deadness, but if the principles above are followed, you will find a way through.

Exercise

Today, use truth as an indicator of your happiness. Truth is a major antidote to feelings of deadness. When something feels dead, truth is being avoided. Happiness is our deepest, truest consciousness; if you are feeling unhappy, it is not the truth. As our problems are resolved, we are led to happiness and as our consciousness grows, so does our happiness. If you are not happy, ask for the truth to be shown to you.

Seek the truth. Desire the truth. It will set you free.

Today, ask for the truth to be shown to you in such a manner you will recognise it and be released. Make truth your ally. Ask to be shown the truth. Listen both within, and to others, and see what the world brings you.

The truth about my relationship with

_____

_____

is:

_____

_____

The truth about my present and past relationships with partners is:

_____

_____

_____

My progress towards my perfect mate or towards my mate becoming my perfect mate is:

_____

_____

WAY 11 Letting Go of the Past Opens up the Present

Once again we have reached a seminal lesson in the process of finding your perfect mate – the principle of letting go. Letting go counters the destructive influence of holding on. Holding on, or attachment, is neediness in the disguise of love. It is a form of counterfeit love that leads to a blurring of personal boundaries between you and the one to whom you are attached. This can lead to urgency and neediness at first, which can set up hurt, unrequited love and conflict. Later, this leads to fusion and sacrifice, which creates feelings of deadness in relationships. The extent of your attachment in relationships is the extent of your unattractiveness, and it repels your partner. What keeps you attractive in a relationship is your letting go of attachment and needs.

But you must distinguish letting go from throwing away, or dissociation. Letting go is a willingness to give up your attachments, so you can feel connection and love with your partner. When your partner becomes independent and needs more space, you are becoming dependent and are called upon to let go. Whenever you let go, your relationship can move forward to the next step in partnership, confidence, and love. Letting go is not throwing away; it is putting in perspective. Letting go is like having the best secretary in the world filing away past papers, so your desk is clear. If anything is needed again you can easily retrieve it.

It is critical to consider letting go to find your perfect mate. If you do not let go of previous relationships, you have barriers in place which will block your ability to begin again, and to go on to the next step. The parts of you or a relationship that you hold onto from your past are prevented from entering your present. In other words, we can hold onto parts of past relationships and, as a result, we are unable to allow these aspects into our present relationships. Think of the good parts of past relationships, of yourself, that you are blocking from having in the present by holding on to the past.

Every anger, hatred, grievance, sadness, and heartbreak you fantasise over and hold on to, prevents you from enjoying yourself. Relationships from the past that may be blocking you include your parent and siblings of the opposite sex. Your attachment to them, which gets in the way of your love for them, blocks you from having a relationship, or limits the quality of that relationship. Joy comes from living in the present – there is no joy living in the past.

At a more conscious level, negative feelings are just an incomplete grieving process. Nobody is fully ready to begin anew until they have let go and finished with, the feelings involved in grieving over the past. At the deepest level of our subconscious, we have these feelings as an attempt to protect ourselves. They are a self-conspiracy we use when we fear the next step. Before the loss occurred, there was always some fear we didn't want to face; and because we didn't face it then, the pain is still within us now. Face it and let it go, because letting go of the pain resolves the fear.

This type of personal conspiracy, subconsciously using pain or problems to keep us from moving forward, is at the heart of all our problems. It is a counter-productive way of dealing with fear because the fear remains. In letting go, the past is resolved. In trust, the present is approached with confidence.

We can never succeed in a relationship without letting go. Letting go is a paradoxical power of the utmost importance in a relationship. When we have need and attachment, we make demands on those around us to handle those needs for us, which drives away those we love and feel we need so much.

Holding on keeps us unattractive. Letting go enhances our attractiveness. Letting go allows everything you prized in past relationships to be available to you in your present or future relationships.

Exercise

Use your intuition as you answer the questions in this exercise. If an answer does not readily occur to you, guess.

Imagine a bucket called 'The Bucket of Relationships'. Estimate the percentage you are holding onto someone, positively or negatively, and drop it into the bucket. For instance, if you are holding on to the parent of the opposite sex at the level of 50 per cent, put that in your bucket. Add 'holdings' with your

*opposite-sex siblings, ex-lovers, favourite fantasy figures
and opposite-sex children if you have any. Your bucket
may begin to look like this:*

> *25 per cent – first love*
> *10 per cent – opposite-sex siblings*
> *20 per cent – opposite-sex parent*
> *5 per cent – favourite star*
> *Total: 60 per cent filled.*

*Even though your bucket starts overflowing, keep on
going till you have listed the last one. It's often the case
that it overflows. Consider your Relationship Bucket
with reference to your present life experience and the
extent of your independence. How full is your bucket?
Its emptiness is the extent to which you are open to a
relationship, or are only open to one of poor quality. The
person in the example above only has the potential for a
40 per cent relationship.*

*I once worked with someone in a workshop whose
bucket was filled to 1,035 per cent. That meant, at
best, she was only able to draw a man who represented
a –935 per cent relationship. It became very clear to her
why she was drawing in such lousy choices for partners.
She made some new choices about letting go and her life
changed for the better.*

*Today is a great day for letting go of old relationships;
here are some ways to do it. Experience any negative
feelings until only a positive feeling is left from the past.
Forgive. Take the next step. Recognise living in the past
is destructive, and choose to live in the present and let
go of old relationships or aspects of them you have held*

onto. Give up attachment, so you can have love. Turn these relationships over to your higher mind to let go for you.

WAY 12 You Can Have What You Want – If You Want What You Have!

Today we will look at two very important concepts: acceptance and letting go.

The title presents a conceptual double meaning about the word 'acceptance'. If you accept what you have, you will automatically and naturally have what you want. It also means that if you do not resist what you have, then what you want can come to you. What you resist persists. When you resist what you have, everything jams and cannot move forward.

Conversely, what you accept changes. Acceptance is not a form of apathy, but an active principle for healing resistance and pain. In some of the most successful chronic pain institutes of North America, people who have had major accidents, suffer from arthritis or other forms of disease are taught to accept and experience their pain, rather than fight it. This simple method is highly effective in lessening pain.

Acceptance gets our lives moving again when they have become stuck; the power of acceptance moves life forward. Sometimes because of hurt, heartbreak, or feelings of rejection, we keep ourselves defended or quit relationships altogether. This locks in the pain. Hurt does not come from what others do or don't do to us. Hurt is the result of how we *react* to what they do. When we finally realise this truth (whether or not someone actually is rejecting us), we can accept that it is our own rejection of ourselves, or our rejection of what they are doing, that creates the hurt. We are in charge of our feelings.

The Buddha's advice for Enlightenment is simple: 'Desire nothing; resist nothing.' We have all heard that we should 'desire nothing', but not many of us realise how important the advice to 'resist nothing' is. Acceptance of reality allows life and relationships to unfold once again.

Letting go is the other key aspect of this important lesson. If you have an expectation, you will stop yourself from moving forward. If you hear yourself saying 'should', 'have to', 'got to', 'need to', 'ought to' or 'must', you have expectations. If you 'need to' or 'have to' have a partner, typically you just can't find one. But paradoxically, when you don't need one, there are plenty around.

Your expectations are demands on others and who wants to feel demands? If you expect things from life you will be frustrated or disappointed. If you don't 'need' something, life often gives you as much of it as you want. Your willingness to give up 'needing' a partner, allows you to have one. Instead, *choose* to have or want a partner. The energy shift your new attitude will bring adds to your attractiveness.

Exercise

Review your life for major hurts.
My list of major hurts:

_____

_____

_____

Choose to accept them rather than deny or hide them,
so that where your life has stopped it can begin to unfold
again. Affirm that being stopped by these old hurts is not
what you want.

Accepting the experience of major difficulties can
actually catapult us into higher consciousness and thus
much greater happiness. Today, turn over to your higher
mind any experience you find impossible to accept. If
you feel hurt, you are in rejection. What is it you have
difficulty accepting?
I have difficulty accepting:

_____

_____

_____

Realise hurt is only a mistake that can be corrected and
does not have to stop you in this area of your life.
What I want now is:

_____

_____

_____

Life is teaching you you don't need anything outside
yourself. Neediness and expectations are two of the

major culprits in chasing partners away. This is not a form of independence, but a way of recognising that your happiness comes from within you. Let go of any feelings of having to have a partner. Trade expectations for a feeling of expectancy. Know your perfect partner is coming your way. Don't make demands and frighten him or her away. Invite your partner in – know your partner is coming. You'll be pleased with the results!

If you have a partner, ask yourself what you are not accepting about them. This is where you are stuck. Choose, even commit, to accept what you have not been accepting with your partner. This will allow your relationship to unfold. Let go of any demands or expectations you have on your partner, so that you can begin receiving. Let go of the expectations and trust – you will be sure to tryst.

WAY 13 Guilt, Unworthiness and Fear Are Merely Illusions

All negative emotions are illusions. Certainly we experience them and they affect us and sometimes even kill us. But, the good news is, these feelings are an illusion. Painful feelings are an indication that something is amiss. I've worked with tens of thousands of people around the world and I have yet to find anyone, with any kind of willingness, who was unable to resolve the blackest guilt, the deepest pain or the greatest fear.

The basis of the mind is happiness, or wholeness and it is that wholeness that allows and promotes our continued movement towards growth and healing. When you penetrate the blocks to your subconscious, unconscious, or even higher mind, you will find yourself in the joy, breakthrough, or ecstasy of transcendence. All negative feelings can be measured against those profoundly happy feelings to evaluate if they are true.

I've encountered many people who thought they were to blame for problem situations in their families while they were growing up, or for other dilemmas they encountered in life. They thought they were so guilty that they did not deserve to have a partner. I've met many others who thought so poorly about themselves they believed they were unworthy of a partner. Others who wanted a partner were afraid to have one, because they felt they were too inadequate to be intimate. They were afraid that when their partners got to know them, they would leave them. The same dynamics will happen within a relationship to keep people in conflict or to keep them apart.

These feelings can be corrected fairly easily. Know that even though you are experiencing such feelings they are not accurate. These feelings, which can block you from finding a partner and destroy relationships, are not the truth. They can be resolved if you are willing to find the way past them and change, so your life can be better.

Exercise

Make a personal inventory of all the negative feelings that may stop you from finding your perfect mate.

Ask your higher mind to show you the way through these feelings or problems.

Choose to drop your guilt. Don't make a monument to a mistake. Don't let mistakes be the superglue that prevents you from moving forward. Choose to correct them. If you are willing to change, a better life awaits you. Choose the truth.

If you give up your 'need' to have the answers, or to have events turn out in a certain way and stop holding on to grievances or negative perceptions, you will experience peace and be free. New answers will come in, as you change your perceptions you will find the whole situation and the people around you will also change.

If you don't feel motivated to make another choice, look for where you are still attached to the pain.

My purpose for holding on to this emotion or problem is:

_____

_____

Do I really want this to hold back my life and happiness?

_____

_____

Now I choose:

_____

_____

WAY 14 Freeing Yourself from Your Life of Fantasy

Here's another important lesson about how you may be blocking yourself from finding your perfect mate or joining your partner at a new level of love. Everyone this side of enlightenment fantasises. There is nothing wrong with fantasising. In fact most human experience takes place in the imagination. When we think we need something, we fantasise. We begin to daydream about it. When we are hungry, we begin to think about food and notice all the cues related to food around us. Fantasy is an attempt to make up for what is missing within or outside you and gives a certain small satisfaction. But it does not really work because it is a defence and all defences cause the very thing you are attempting to defend yourself against. In this case, it creates no reality, only fantasy. To your mind, everything is a picture. Your mind cannot distinguish between you actually doing something and just thinking about it. So, if you are having sex, or merely imagining you are having sex, your mind does not know the difference.

If you fantasise about your perfect mate, you will often give yourself enough satisfaction; you won't bother to open yourself up for a real relationship. You can create a level of dissatisfaction within a relationship with the continued use of fantasy.

Fantasy is using your imagination to make up for something missing. The more you fantasise, the more illusions you place between yourself and your partner. As your partner cannot live up to your fantasies, a growing sense of dissatisfaction, disappointment and frustration becomes inevitable. Be careful: if you let fantasy grow in your relationship, your attempts to make your partner more exciting will actually push your partner away because they will never be enough.

Fantasy is a compensation for loss, pain, grievance and the judgement that something is missing in your life. Fantasy is an attempt to provide something that can only be achieved by joining with your partner at a new level of intimacy. Fantasy hides the crucial need to take the next step. When you fantasise, you are stuck and attempting to be satisfied by an illusion. Ultimately it won't work. Let go of your fantasies so you can experience the real thing in a way that satisfies you.

Whether or not you have a partner, your ego steps in every now and then to offer a dose of fantasy. You are encouraged to fantasise about a lost partner or even an 'ideal' partner which does, of course, place a wedge between you and any potential partner, or even between you and the partner you have at present. The dissatisfaction engendered by fantasy can lead you to drop your present partner. Then, when you move forward to a new relationship, your ego plays its tricks again, only this time you have two relationships to fantasise about. The fantasy accelerates and sets up disappointment all over again.

Exercise

When you catch yourself in a fantasy today, find out what is underneath it. Somewhere it is hiding a painful feeling which is acting as a wedge between you and your partner.

Let go of any painful feeling by experiencing it until it is complete, or by handing it over to your higher mind.

Recognise the pain for which your fantasies are compensating before turning them, especially those involving your perfect mate, over to your higher self.

My fantasy:

_____

_____

The pain or need it was hiding was:

_____

_____

I am ready for the next step!

WAY 15 If it Hurts, it isn't Love

Contrary to many popular and traditional songs, love does not hurt, but 'needs' do. Your past heartbreaks were really frustrations of your needs – part of a power struggle, where you used your hurt as a form of emotional blackmail to force your partner to do what you wanted and meet your needs. Your heartbreaks are really acts of revenge through which your pain declares the true, terrible character of your partner.

When you understand the dynamics of hurt and rejection you can take a giant stride towards maturity and you will open up to relationships, and to being a better partner, once you find your mate. Hurt is an attempt to make someone wrong. It results from something you cannot accept, that you resist, or reject. What you push away from you creates the hurt and emotional pain. Then you project the pushing away on to your partner and feel rejected. Projection is a defence. Projection is taking something you are doing and accusing someone else of doing it. Hurt results from giving to take, a form of sacrifice used to coerce your partner. When your partner pushes you away for taking, you get upset, which hides what you are doing. Using hurt or heartbreak as part of your conspiracy to gain control and thus do what you want can be harmful to you both in finding a relationship and keeping one healthy.

Exercise

If you have any experience which still hurts, discover the control that hurt is giving you. Would you rather have that control, or the perfect mate? Would you rather have the hurt that breeds more hurt and dependence, or a happy, sharing relationship?
My experiences that still hurt:

_____

_____

Through this hurt I am controlling:

_____

_____

Control is the part of independence that leads to fights. It is universally unattractive except to those looking for someone to take care of their needs. The openness of intimacy is rich and attractive to others. Openness may be a risk but it is also the excitement and ability to enjoy. Your change is your cure.
What I really want:

_____

_____

I will be happy when I have:

_____

_____

Trust is one of the cornerstones of a relationship. There is no love without trust. Trust is the opposite of naivety, which is denial parading as innocence. When you trust you turn the power of your mind towards that which you are trusting, in an attitude of confidence, power and success. Trust is one of the core healing principles. Trust can resolve any problem. A problem comes about because, given the nature of your subconscious, your mind is split. Whenever you are hurt in a major way, you fragment a piece of your mind and reject that part as painful. The fragmented part is projected outward and comes back to meet you as the problem. When this happens you adopt an attitude of control to keep the pain away from you. When you put trust into a negative situation, it begins to work for you and the situation unfolds in a positive way. Control is a subtle form of power struggle that blocks relationships and indicates a fear of intimacy. It is the opposite of trust. Control attempts to take into its own power that which trust brings about by opening things up and clearing the way for resolution.

Exercise

Today, every time you think of your perfect mate, know

your perfect mate is coming to you. Trust yourself and your partner. As you put trust into your present relationship, it will unfold as you do.

Possibly there is a part of you which wants a relationship and another which is afraid to have one. Or a part that wants to move forward in your present relationship and a part that is frightened. Imagine holding these two parts, one in each hand. Feel their weight and texture. See or sense their colour, size and shapes. Smell their aromas. Hear any sounds they make.

Imagine they are melting down to their pure energy – the basic building block of the universe. Notice that when they are completely melted down the two handfuls are exactly the same. Join the two handfuls of energy, so that when they are completely joined your fingers are interlocked. Notice the new feeling, or form, emerging from the integration gives you your mind back – whole. If any bad feelings remain, reintegrate them with the whole just created and with your higher mind.

Repeat this exercise as often as necessary to heal all the layers involved. As the inside progresses to peace and wholeness, the outside transforms to success.

WAY 17 Manifesting Your Life

This is one of the three most important seminal lessons in finding your perfect mate. Do it well! To manifest something we simply choose what we want to happen. We do it all the time subconsciously. People who are good at manifesting what they want are those who know they have the power and use it consciously. Everything, including the negative stuff, happens because we choose it. Today's lesson could change the rest of your life if you make this principle a part of your life.

When I was young and single and thought that fun was dating different women, I used to make lists of the attributes I wanted in my woman. The lists were long and specific describing characteristics, time available, etc., so that it would take months for my exact order to come to me. But she always did come with those specific details. If I had been more mature I might have been able to feel and enjoy those relationships more.

Manifesting is choosing to have something occur and it does. You could be choosing what you want to have happen at any time of day. The times the mind is most receptive is in the twilight sleep zones: just before you fall asleep and just before you get up. That's the time to tell yourself the kinds of feelings and experiences you want to have during the coming day or in the near future. If you find something occurs which you do not like, then choose your preference again. If something negative happens, then: acknowledge that you did not want it, acknowledge that you made a subconscious if not a conscious mistake in your choice, realise you deserve better outcomes, know if it's unhappy it is not the truth, choose once again what you want, and turn it over to your higher self.

This one principle could keep you in happiness for the rest of your life. Choose situations in which everyone wins, and keep your integrity. Never choose someone else's partner, because that would create problems, guilt and delay for all concerned. And you might miss out on someone meant specifically for you. Your true partner will come to you unencumbered.

Remember to manifest happy things like health and abundance for those around you. What you manifest for others is manifested for you. How you bless others is how you are blessed.

Exercise

List the qualities you want in your partner:

_____

_____

_____

_____

I choose to recognise my perfect mate as they show up.
  Leave it open enough for anything else that your

higher mind might want to include for your happiness. Experience the energy of your request, how good it feels and send it out into the universe, knowing your partner will soon be there. Any time you think of your partner, know your partner is coming to you. Have gratitude both for what you have and what is coming. Don't worry about not doing it exactly right. It is not the way that you do it which counts, but your intention. I've heard of at least half a dozen ways of doing this and they all worked. This is the essence. When you have finished let your higher mind handle it for you. You may develop a style that works better for you. Trust yourself. And good luck.

If you are in a relationship, you can manifest a new stage in your relationship – a breakthrough, a romance step, a long romance step, deep love, a new understanding, an argument healed, progress made, a step taken, love renewed, a lucky night, a joyful weekend, a fun night, a heartfelt talk, a great vacation and much more. Your only limits are your own imagination. You can also manifest increased maturity and the ability to receive and enjoy each other. The sky is the limit. This is a great tool to keep your relationship alive and growing.

WAY 18   Your Attitude is Your Direction

Your attitude is the most fundamental aspect of your life because it defines your direction. Your attitude is made up of your decisions, all moving in the same general direction. It's important to know what you want, where you want to go, to set goals and make good decisions to support that goal (and you may have to be courageous and take a few risks). You will need to change for you to have your perfect mate, or even for you to be happy with your perfect mate. Change is inevitable if you want to succeed, because – just think for a moment – if you go on doing what you've been doing, you'll go on getting more of what you've already got. Your attitude towards change is crucial to your success. If you are in pain, or feeling the deadness, you may begin to recognise change as the greatest blessing on earth. Why don't you just decide that any change will be exciting or a great adventure? It is important to choose not only to have your perfect mate, but to be happy and reach wholeness with him or her. This may seem obvious, but without choosing that second goal your first major misunderstanding may be your last. Once you have chosen your goal for the relationship anything which comes up is just something to work out on your way to happiness.

There are problems and situations to work on and heal in every relationship. Everything between you and total joy will come up between you and your partner, because old pain and behaviour patterns disguise themselves as problems in present relationships and lead us into fights or deadness. So have a healing attitude in your relationship. If anything is not love, it is a call for help, a call for your understanding. This thought helps us look beyond negative behaviour to what is underneath and respond with love and understanding. When you find your perfect mate, believe me, the journey is just beginning.

Romance is the first stage in a relationship. It is swiftly followed by two phases that need joining and healing to enjoy the breakthrough and romance: the Power Struggle and the Dead Zone before you move into Co-creation. Many relationships don't make it through the Dead Zone. Major falling outs and breakups happen during the Power Struggle. Your attitude towards and understanding of these stages is crucially important to help your relationship thrive. Choose to become an expert in intimacy, love, communication, trust, letting go and forgiveness. Then, not only will your relationship move forward, your whole life may move forward in leaps and bounds. Decide your relationship will be about more than just you and your feelings, but about truth and healing. That choice alone could save you from years of dead ends and delays in which you are subtly, or not so subtly, taking control or making *you* the most important part of your relationship. Given the complexity of the human mind, there are literally thousands of things of a very complicated nature and simple things of profound dimensions to heal in a relationship. They can all be healed (and simply) if there is true desire and a willingness to move forward.

Step by step, your ease and confidence will grow as you mature. Choose to learn your relationship lessons quickly and easily. Make sure your partner always wins 100 per cent alongside you. If you don't, you will end up paying the bill, by sacrifice or by loss of your partner's attractiveness. Choose to learn joyfully and remove the ways that separate you and your partner.

Exercise

Take a long look at your life. Where are you heading? It's time to change, to work to eliminate choices, prejudices, or fear which may be holding you back.

Choose goals and attitudes for your relationship that will support your use of this most powerful vehicle of healing for your mutual growth and happiness. Commit to them.

My new goals and attitudes are:

_____

_____

I deserve the best!

WAY 19 Free Your Family, Free Yourself

After years of researching what sets up life patterns and the seemingly never-ending self-generating wellsprings of guilt that flood out of the subconscious mind, a number of things have become evident to me. Guilt blocks abundance and receiving, simultaneously generating self-attack and attacks and problems that seem to come from the outside world. No matter how much is cleared, there always seems to be more and more guilt. Guilt is a major dynamic in all problems, including scarcity, but the more innocent we recognise ourselves to be, the easier and more abundant our life gets. Over the years I've learned there are areas in the subconscious where guilt seems to come up layer after layer, stopping people from growth and generating negative life patterns. I discovered these patterns begin in the family and often begin with experiences in the womb. I became aware of a number of dynamics common to these events.

The first is that these events become part of our personal conspiracies to stop our own greatness, our personal purpose and our relationship purpose. We get frightened of the next step in our unfolding and when we are about to take that step we subconsciously manifest a drama which blocks us. Typically, this is (or was) a trauma which involves members of our family.

Over two decades of therapy, I discovered that we seem to have come *to heal the very problems or situations that traumatised us*. We are the grace bringers – the gift-givers – by which I mean we have the ability through our 'beingness' to heal the problems that trap us in our families. When we are in a state of 'beingness' things work out, but when we blame others or ourselves or get trapped into feelings of sacrifice, we fail. And then we work harder, do more, compensate, to try to prove we are good and successful people. Unfortunately, we become caught up by the very problems and uneasiness that we came to heal. Typically, in the face of some overwhelming family problem, we begin to blame ourselves rather than recognise the gift we came to deliver.

Specifically, we came to save each of our family members, our parents as a couple and our family as a whole. Each child comes in to help and support the child who has come before in a sort of res-cue mission. Yet this is typically misunderstood by us. Research shows the birth of a sibling can be one of the most painful experiences a person goes through in life, rather than the welcoming of a friend and ally.

As children, we began to blame ourselves. We leave our centre to try to resolve the problems of our family. When we left our centres, we entered illusion and sacrifice, taking on a 'job' in an attempt to help. This 'job' is something we feel we have to do for someone in the family, like making them happy, or making lots of money for them or stopping them being angry. We may be enslaved or rebel against doing it, but we are caught by it. As soon as we left our centres we left our natural boundaries and fused with family members, setting up sacrifice and guilt as a way of life.

Unfortunately we could never succeed at the job and that generated feelings of failure and guilt. Out of fear we 'do' the job ourselves rather than allowing it to be done through grace or just through our beingness. Repeatedly we left our centres, that place of innocence and simplicity, unaware that it could lead to self-destruction and even death of that self. We compensated for our failure and guilt by 'doing' more to prove we have value. However, since this is only a form of proving, we could not let ourselves receive our gift.

The mind, being resilient, willingly begins a new self for us, but begins it from off our centre, in a guilty, unreceiving place. Blaming ourselves, feeling guilty, we go off our centres trying to make the problem better by our sacrifice. This leads to taking on a 'job', doingness, compensation for the guilt by hard work. This causes difficulty, fusion and competition in our lives. When I finally understood this dynamic, the solution looked simple. It works this way. With the help of the higher mind (as the process could take weeks or even months without it) we can be carried back into our centres. Each of our family members can at our request be carried back to their centres.

Returning to our centres resolves long-standing guilt and removes negative life patterns. Since the purpose of guilt is to stop us moving forward, those guilt-related blocks produce life patterns that stop our personal purpose. Once these blocks are resolved in our families, then we can naturally give our gift to the world. If your self has 'died', imagine breathing life back into it so it can come alive again. Then it can be carried back into your centre and be reintegrated.

Your gift is not necessarily something you do. It is something you embody naturally. It proceeds in grace from your being and creates more ease and success in your life. It is something that is naturally shared by your being and your presence. When we cover this gift with a conspiracy of guilt and failure, we set up a family of other conspiracies.

Exercise

List the major grievances you have towards people in your family, both living and dead:

_____

_____

This is what you came to help them with and even save them from. Each grievance stops you unfolding and your natural movement forward. These grievances hide your guilt and lock you into sacrifice in some form of unsuccessful pattern. So be willing to forgive the person with whom you had a grievance by not using that person to hold yourself back.

Imagine taking the hand of each person you had a

grievance with and see yourself walking forward, arm in arm, into the next stage of your life. You are no longer stuck with your grievances, each step will realise a gift that has been waiting for you since the grievance began. Imagine yourself giving the gift that was hidden under your grievance, sacrifice and guilt. It can still free you. As you go forward you will have layer after layer of gifts to free you and your family. You will begin to see everything around you improve – bit by bit – as you give these gifts. What you thought was chronic and impossible to change finally begins to change. This process will work even if the person has died because it has a freeing effect on the life and karmic patterns of everyone involved and re-establishes personal value.

I am becoming free!

WAY 20   Roles, Rules and Duties

Roles and duties are about doing the right things for the wrong reasons. We drop into roles for approval, perform our expected duties to prove we are good and to show others, usually our parents, how they should have acted in order to treat us right. Roles and duties are based on grievances, feelings of guilt and failure. They are embodied forms of sacrifice and compensate us for our painful feelings. Roles are like suits of armour encasing us, cutting us off from intimacy, from our ability to give and receive. Roles create deadness. The two most common roles are 'being good' and 'being a hard worker'.

In our society, the age at which most trauma happens appears to be about three years old, when we take on most of our roles. Roles and duties are aspects of character. They are strategies we develop as children to help us compensate for our feelings of failure and guilt. Later these roles can actually kill an adult by creating a deep-seated exhaustion that becomes burn-out. A child is naturally flexible, loving, creative, giving, receiving and authentic. This openness cannot exist when you are acting out roles and neither can commitment, truth, ease, freedom and the other qualities that bring on success. Interestingly enough, fear of commitment is actually a fear of sacrifice, which results from living out roles, 'doing what is expected even if I don't like it'. Paradoxically, true commitment creates freedom, release and ease because it emerges from choice and total giving. Giving and receiving increase our sense of self-worth and heal the main dynamic of fear of commitment (which is that no one, including ourselves, is worthy of continuous attention). Giving and receiving naturally integrate opposites, bringing about the light.

Rules are built on guilt and pain. They have the same dynamics as roles and duties. They are rigid demands on ourselves and others, which lead to no-win situations, because if someone follows your rules, you feel a bit safer but still have the fear that generated those rules. Rules are counterfeit principles.

Principles flow and are life generating, beginning dialogue not ending it. Each of us has hundreds of contradictory rules about relationships. They are our attempts to keep ourselves safe but, in the end, they separate us from our loved ones. Since rules are made to be broken, they bring about the very things they were meant to prevent.

Exercise

Look for all the areas in which you are giving, but don't seem to be receiving. Giving and receiving is a natural cycle, giving leads to receiving. An area where you are not receiving is an area in which you are in a role. To change a role into true giving just choose *to give rather than giving because you are supposed to.*

The areas in which I am giving and not receiving:

_____
_____
_____
_____

Make a list of all your rules which apply to the areas where you would feel hurt, upset or insulted if your rules weren't kept, e.g. infidelity, tardiness, insensitivity. To find these rules, think back to the times you felt hurt. As you find your rules, make new choices about the ones you feel ready to let go of. Turn those rules over to your higher mind to change into principles. A rule is rigid but a principle is flexible, which may be why people say that 'rules are meant to be broken'. A rule hides old pain and guilt and is really a defence begging to be attacked so that the pain and guilt can be healed. Typically, when a rule is broken and we experience pain in a relationship, we adopt a reactive, defensive or attacking posture to protect ourselves rather than using the opportunity for communication, healing and evolution.
My rules are:

_____
_____
_____
_____

Look closely at your roles or rules that may be preventing you from having a relationship.
The roles I am willing to change:

_____
_____

The rules I am willing to change:

_____

_____

_____

I am making good choices!

WAY 21 Family Roles

Family roles can stop you having your perfect mate. They can block many of the good things in life. The major family roles are the hero, the martyr, the scapegoat, the lost child and the charmer. The hero, martyr and scapegoat are all guilt induced, while the charmer and the lost child are generated by feelings of inadequacy. The hero is the shining light in the family, always succeeding, always winning, being good at sports, getting excellent grades, etc. The hero is the person in the family of whom everyone is proud. Heroes are trying to save the family by being the very best. Unfortunately, it is only a compensation for feeling guilty. The scapegoat is the problem person in the family, always in lots of trouble. Scapegoats attempt to help the family by bringing all the troubles of the family on their own shoulders and trying to save it through their calls for help to outside agencies such as the police. They try to distract the family from its problems. This is their contribution to the family and it is a compensation for guilt. The martyr works hard, becomes sick or has problems in an attempt to swallow everyone's pain and save the family. Martyrs are a cross between hero and scapegoat, sacrificing themselves in an unsuccessful attempt to save the family.

The next two roles, the lost child and the charmer,

emerge from feelings of inadequacy. The lost child doesn't feel good enough to be wanted and thinks the best way to help the family is by disappearing or becoming invisible. Charmers, or mascots, entertain the family with their humour and play. Yet underneath they feel as though they are not valued for who they are, but only for what they do for people. Entertaining everyone, they believe, is their best contribution to the family.

All these roles are forms of giving without receiving. A family apportions different jobs to its members in an unsuccessful attempt to find balance and save itself. The more a family is caught up in roles, the more dysfunctional it is; and the more dysfunctional a family is, the more it will get caught in roles. It is a vicious circle.

A family is a unit. It has a 'group mind', so that at a subconscious level every role and action of family members is a family decision. Every member in the family is co-responsible. From what I have seen in my years of working in therapy, it seems that our family dynamics actually generate the subconscious mind. Unless we are transformed, the family roles are with us for our lifetime. Although we play all the roles in our family, we normally concentrate on one or two in our lives. These roles can interfere with forming a relationship. A martyr might be refusing to find a partner because of having to take care of the family or an aged parent. A scapegoat might be so caught up in the role of getting into trouble to save the family that his or her own life may be on hold. Until you consciously rid yourself of your family role, or you are living at a visionary level, you are caught up in this dynamic. The roles we play become part of our relationships and sooner or later the guilt and sense of failure that led us to play them in our family will surface in our relationship.

Within a relationship, these family roles are both unsuccessful and maintain levels of separation, deadness and fraudulence. Choose to let these go to generate new intimacy in your relationship. Family roles also create deadness by blocking authenticity. Healing ourselves from family roles is important in order to get rid of the sacrifice that scares us away from relationships. It helps to create the freedom that allows for commitment, partnership and intimacy. Being locked in our family roles never allows us fully to grow up.

Exercise

Take a look at your family. Which roles does everyone play? If you catch yourself in a role, you can make another choice.

Be willing to make other choices if these roles are not serving you but realise there can be many layers to these roles. As you find a new balance, your family will too.

Every role is a place where you are off your centre. Ask your higher mind to carry you back to your centre and when you feel a greater sense of peace, ask that your family be carried back to your family's centre. Repeat this until it feels totally peaceful, going down to deeper centres. Don't use your family as an excuse to stay stuck. As you move forward, it will benefit everyone in your family and your life. Family roles and family patterns are among the worst traps to stop you living your purpose and being happy.

Be willing to learn your lessons and not to use anyone or anything to hold yourself back.

I will use no one and nothing to hold me back from having my perfect love.

WAY 22 Nothing is Hard if You Really Want it

'Nothing is hard if you really want it' is another way of saying commitment opens you up to receive everything you want. I have dealt with this concept a good number of times in hundreds of seminars and workshops. Usually it is fear, guilt, unworthiness, loss or sacrifice that prevents people having what they want. There is always some kind of ambivalence present: if you were not ambivalent you would have your true partner.

From observing the dynamics of thousands of people, one of the core reasons we don't allow ourselves to have it all – love, money, sex, success, etc. – is because we would be embarrassed to win so much and be so successful. We are afraid of having to deal with envy and so too often we give up on our gifts and talents. We literally make ourselves smaller to fit in with the rest of the crowd. But having given up our natural gifts and thus having surrendered our leadership qualities and uniqueness, we still want to be special in everyone else's eyes. We become competitive, trying to keep our partners small so we are not threatened by their greatness and then attacking them if they don't treat us specially enough. We demand the acknowledgement and attention from others that we are not giving ourselves or our partners and so it goes on and on. Every single one of us has fallen into this trap.

Many chapters could be written about specialness. Suffice it to say for now that we mistakenly want our specialness more than we want love. Specialness is a counterfeit love that causes hurt when we are not treated specially enough in the way we want. If you want something totally and focus the full power of your mind on it, natural success will follow often in unexpected ways. Using the full power of your mind can open the door to abundance in every area of your life.

My wife, when she was my live-in girlfriend, accurately thought I had a fear of commitment. But at the suggestion of a friend of ours, she decided to 'choose me'. For three days, she wrestled with her own fear of commitment that had not surfaced before. After burning away the fear, she was ready to commit to me. Paradoxically and simultaneously, as she was choosing me I was at the same time choosing her. We learned the power of really wanting something and choosing it in spite of apparent blocks.

There is a great quotation from Goëthe that really speaks of the power of wholly wanting something:

Until one is committed there is hesitancy.
The chance to draw back.
Always ineffectiveness.
Concerning all acts of initiative (and creation)
There is one elementary truth.
The ignorance of which kills countless ideas and splendid
    plans:
That the moment one definitely commits oneself

Then Providence moves, too.
All sorts of things occur to help one
That would never otherwise have occurred.
A whole stream of events issues from the decision
Raising in one's favour
All manner of unforeseen incidents and meetings
   and material assistance,
Which no man would have dreamt would have come
   his way.
Whatever you can do, or dream you can, begin
   it.
Boldness has genius, power, and magic in it.
BEGIN IT NOW.

Johann Wolfgang von Goëthe

Commitment is the gift of opportunity we give ourselves.

Exercise

Today, let's re-examine ambivalence. Answer the following questions and as answers or thoughts come to you intuitively write them down.
What specifically holds you back from having your true partner?

_____

_____

What style do you have that chases partners away?

_____

_____

What is it you are afraid of?

_____

_____

What do you think you would lose if you got a partner?

_____

_____

What do you feel too guilty about to have your true partner?

_____

_____

Why don't you deserve your true partner?

_____

_____

Who would be too jealous of you if you got your perfect partner?

_____

_____

Any answer that came up is not the truth! It is a belief you have used against yourself to stop you. You can choose to change these beliefs. You can change them with the help of your higher mind. Practise really wanting your perfect mate (not 'needing', but wanting). If any feelings come up which block this, experience them through until they are complete and a feeling of expectancy is present.

I want my partner more than fear, lack of confidence or anything else that is blocking me.

I commit to having my true love.

I commit to having true love with my partner.

WAY 23   Healing Power Struggles

Power struggles are the major stumbling block to an unfolding relationship. If a couple does not learn how to transcend their power struggles, they are unlikely to succeed in their relationship. Many people are afraid of venturing into a committed relationship because they do not think they will survive the fighting, or deadness, caused by competition, which is a subtle form of power struggle. When I finally decided, at the ripe old age of thirty-six, to commit to one relationship as my best chance for happiness, it was only because I finally felt I had learned and healed enough to have a good chance of success without fighting. If you understand the dynamics of power struggles, you will know what to do to succeed. Awareness is half the battle.

In power struggles, we typically make the biggest mistake in a relationship. We think the other person has been put on earth solely for the purpose of taking care of our needs. We cover this up during the romance stage, but it emerges in force in the power struggle stage when we fight to have things done our way, which we believe is the 'right way'. We give our partners an ultimatum to do it 'my way or take to the highway'. We fight for control. We fight to be the most independent one. We fight to have our needs met first, or twice if our partner is not too tired. A power struggle is a fight to get our partners to meet our needs. We are so afraid to do it our partner's way because we were hurt, even devastated, as children, when we did it the very way our partner wants us to do it now. We vowed never to do anything like that again so we could not be devastated. For us to do it the way our partner requests can seem like a question of life or death because of the old feelings.

There are a number of ways to resolve this, but one of the easiest is to realise that every competition, every power struggle, is a delaying tactic. It delays the moment when we step forward to resolve the issue and have the needs of both partners healed. In these fights each person looks to the other to fulfil needs that would be best filled by stepping forward. If you win, if you beat your partner and get your needs met, your partner loses – which means you end up paying the price because as your partner loses, he or she correspondingly becomes less attractive, which means you lose. If your partner loses, he or she goes into sacrifice and a level of deadness is introduced into the relationship, which again means you are the loser. If you are not committed to both of you winning 100 per cent, you will find yourself losing to the same extent your partner does.

When your relationship is in trouble, or when your partner is moving away from you, you are usually in the throes of a power struggle. Even if you have reached higher levels in your relationship, it is possible to have been tripped up by this most fundamental lesson of all relationships. You are, in effect, flunking the basic lesson of a relationship.

You are dependent and in denial about your part in the drama. You are trying to use your partner in order to get your own needs met. This and this alone keeps them moving away from you, keeps you unattractive and lacking integrity. Only as you let go will all of this change. Only then can you win back your attractiveness (in your own eyes and theirs) and, of course, their love.

It is important to be brutally honest with yourself. Whining and complaining mask the fact that you are not taking responsibility, or seeing how your dependency is chasing them away. Burn these needy, painful feelings. Give them to your higher mind. Step forward in your life. Give up seeing your partner as someone who will save you. Let go of your attachment or you will lose your partner and your relationship. If you are willing to learn this lesson, your higher mind will guide you. If you stay in denial, being false to yourself and always trying to take, you will undoubtedly chase your partner away. The results do not lie. You might hide what you are doing from yourself, but it will show in the results. This is the most basic step in a power struggle. If your relationship has regressed back to this, it is time to learn this lesson. Totally committing to your partner is the easiest way through this, if you have the courage. But if you lie to yourself about this, they will move away and you will suffer. Don't use power struggles as a means to protect the fear that both of you feel, and to keep you both from stepping forward to the next life change. Say 'YES!' to life, so you can move forward easily and fully along with your partner.

Exercise

Think carefully about anyone you are fighting with, or fought with in the past.
What step forward were you afraid of?

_____

_____

_____

What was the gift, or the new level, you turned away from out of fear?

_____

_____

_____

That step, that gift, that new level is still there for you. Be willing to receive this gift or new level for yourself and for all those you love. The step you take is given to your partner through grace.
Who am I fighting with?

_____

_____

What am I afraid of?

_____

_____

I deserve the best!

Transforming Boredom

Boredom stops relationships! People are afraid of commitment to a relationship for fear of dying a slow and painful death from boredom. *Boredom is easily resolved by taking an emotional risk in communication or intimacy with your partner!* Such risks create new levels of emotional and sexual excitement.

Often when we begin a relationship, we spend the first couple of years, or however long, giving our partners all the gifts we have to give. But at some point the gifts run out and we feel bankrupt with nothing left to give our partners. In the next phase of the relationship what we can give our partners is our pain. If we give our pain saying 'I give this pain to you so it will no longer come between us', it becomes a major contribution showing confidence in the relationship and leads to greater intimacy and excitement. But when we withhold ourselves, usually from fear because we are trying to keep ourselves safe, we end up bored.

The biggest source of boredom in a relationship comes from sacrifice masquerading as love. Everybody has confused sacrifice with love. Sacrifice is counterfeit love. The sacrificer gives, but does not receive. Love is naturally giving and receiving. Giving without receiving leads to 'burn-out' and deadness. Receiving leads to giving at a whole new level. We go into sacrifice behaviour because we don't value ourselves. At those times when our self-esteem is low we think sacrifice, giving up our own wants and desires, time and money, is the only thing we can offer our partner. It looks to us as if sacrifice, which is a form of self-punishment, is one of the best ways of paying off guilt. So we give ourselves up and use the other's self to carry us forward, but as we do so we lose the points of contact and intimacy that bring excitement and joy to a relationship.

Sacrifice is a form of passive aggression, since withdrawal of contact and withholding is just as deadly as attack. When we complain someone has 'used us', the truth is we used them in order to avoid moving forward.

Sacrifice does not work and bogs down a relationship. It is a form of compromise or adjustment to a situation that needs healing, or resolving, through open and honest communication, otherwise both partners will feel they have lost.

Exercise

What communications are you withholding from your partner and/or your last partner?
I did not tell them:

_____

_____

_____

Be willing to risk sharing those feelings. They are your

feelings. You are responsible for them. They can only change if you share them intending to heal yourself. If you try to use them to emotionally control someone into doing things your way – it won't work!

Sometimes in a relationship you are afraid to share your experiences, thoughts and feelings because you think they will devastate your partner. But these are the very things that are killing the relationship. Because you are withholding them, you keep things safe and create deadness. For instance, if you tell your partner you are no longer sexually attracted to him or her, it is either the end of the relationship, or the moment when you accept the risk and reach for a new level of communication. It is taking responsibility for feelings of upset and deadness that must be healed if you, or the relationship, are to survive. What we withhold are the very issues that must be resolved for our relationships to grow. Paradoxically, sharing these private and important things and moving past them together can make a relationship exciting again.

All sacrifice is based on past and present grievances, against someone you felt did not do it right for you. Your sacrifice is an attempt to show how it should have been done. List all the sacrifice situations you can remember from when you were a child right up to today so you can discover the hidden grievances. Forgive them so you can both be free.

Sacrifice in the present is a way of avoiding what you are frightened to face. For example:

Sacrifice – I always do things for my boyfriend that I don't want to do or give.

Present grievance – I feel used.

Past grievance – I blame my mother: she always told me I was good when I was doing things for her I didn't want to do.

The trap – I am afraid I have no self-worth because I am afraid to use my creativity.

The excuse it gave me – I used my mother and boyfriend to give me an excuse not to face my creativity.

The solution – communicate, forgive, choose:

Communicate: *Let those people know you feel you are in sacrifice to them but take responsibility for it and don't blame them. Remember your sacrifice is a form of using them to hold yourself back.*

Forgive: *Forgive everyone involved, because forgiveness will heal both of you. Ask for the help of your higher mind and say, 'I forgive [say his or her name], so that we may both be free.'*

Choose: *Those areas where you feel role, duty or sacrifice can be turned into pure giving by choosing to give freely rather than doing it because you are supposed to.*

WAY 25   Commitment: The Gateway to Freedom

I would like to introduce a notion which single independent people don't even begin to suspect and which people in committed relationships know: commitment brings a freedom that generates truth and ease. Independent people are afraid commitment is a kind of slavery. The spectre of sacrifice is one of the major reasons, ranking alongside heartbreak and jealousy, why people stay single, carefully guarding their independence. Unfortunately, being independent solves nothing – it only hides problems. We can be independent or inter-dependent. The extent to which we choose independence rather than inter-dependence is the measure of how much we were heartbroken and in sacrifice when we were dependent. It is also the extent to which we are afraid of intimacy.

When we lose our natural bonding in relationships we tend to drop into sacrifice, or fusion, to simulate intimacy. Sometimes the old pain under that sacrifice, or fusion, waits till a new relationship begins and resurfaces to be healed. Bonding, the natural connectedness and cohesiveness of love, nurtures and protects us and by healing the deadness in relationships we can re-enter the natural joyous state that bonding brings. Commitment brings freedom into existence leading a couple into the truth and ease of real partnership. Miraculously, because a relationship is a team effort and the success of one is enjoyed by both, it only takes one partner to choose commitment to move the couple on to the next step in partnership.

Commitment has the power to shift some of the biggest conflicts in a relationship. Let me explain. Right after the honeymoon or romance stage we reach the first unpleasant form of power struggle called the shadow stage. This looks like one of the biggest shifts in a relationship. Suddenly our perspective changes and we go from seeing our partner as heaven-sent to seeing them as a spectre from hell. Our partner becomes our worst nightmare because we are projecting our greatest fears onto them. We want to get away – to distance ourselves. This is the moment when we think they have changed for the worst. 'You are not the person I married,' we moan. But the truth is we are punishing them for the problems buried within ourselves, never for theirs. We are punishing them for crimes we feel we have committed and mistakes we feel we have made. Commitment does not often spring to mind when we have this negative experience of our partner, but if we re-commit to them at this point, those evil shadows that were scaring us disappear and we step forward into greater partnership having learned the next major lesson about relationships.

Another time when major change seems to occur is when a couple has passed through their power struggle stage into that of the Dead Zone. This is a particularly difficult time, full of illusions and pitfalls. Feelings of love and sexual attraction both seem to fall away and sometimes are replaced with a feeling of revulsion or repulsion towards our partner. Choosing your partner then in that time of darkness paradoxically changes both your experience of them and the relationship itself for the better.

Commitment is prioritising. It is giving of ourselves fully so that we receive fully. Because commitment makes your partner more important than your needs and your conflicts, it resolves them. Together with trust, forgiveness and a number of other major healing choices, commitment has the power to shift any problem completely.

Exercise

Today, adopt a new attitude towards commitment because it is what you give in any situation that determines your experience of it. When you give the best of yourself in a relationship you will feel you are the one who is having the best.

Choose a situation, or person, with whom you seem to be in conflict, or where you feel deadness.

I seem to be in conflict with:

_____

_____

_____

Decide to give 100 per cent to that person or situation and witness the change. You'll know how much you have given by how the relationship enlivens. Our partners never fail unless we stop giving to them.

I choose to commit myself fully to my life by giving myself 100 per cent to the people and the situations that are important to me.

WAY 26 As You Believe, So Shall it Be

Nothing can happen to you unless you believe it can. Our beliefs make up a matrix that we project out on to the world, which returns looking as if it is what is really happening in the world. If you change your mind you can literally change the world.

In my work as a therapist and marriage counsellor I have seen people time and again producing immense change in seemingly impossible situations by applying this principle. When you understand how it works, it's no longer necessary to work at adjusting or changing the outside situation. Instead you only need find and change the subconscious pattern of belief to accelerate the healing process and put the power of transformation back in your own hands. It gives you the power to get out of one of life's biggest traps: believing that you are a victim.

When I learned this, I experienced some major breakthroughs and insights regarding my own life. The block I had in writing my doctoral dissertation fell away when I correctly identified the subconscious thought that both my parents, who were divorced, would come to my doctoral graduation and somehow get back together again. I realised I was not just writing a dissertation, which was difficult enough, but I was also trying to do the seemingly impossible and bring my family back together. Suddenly I understood why I had nearly died a number of years earlier and what had led me to almost quit my life. My near-death experience was a subconscious last-ditch attempt, by sacrificing myself, to bring my family back together because I blamed myself for what had happened in my family.

Discovering and examining our beliefs is one of the easiest ways to get into our subconscious to change it. In any situation ask yourself intuitively 'What do I believe that could make this happen?' Your intuitive mind is a far better tool for this purpose than your analytical mind because it allows information to pop into your mind. For instance, if your partner has treated you badly, ask yourself 'What must I believe about my partner, relationships and the opposite sex that this could happen?' Your feelings originate from your beliefs, thoughts, and values. If you believe the opposite sex will reject you, then you are probably overly self-conscious around them because you are afraid of being rejected yet again!

But here's the bad news, the nature of fear is that whatever you fear you are already feeling. So if you are afraid of rejection, you are feeling rejected. When you feel rejected you act rejected, and that leads to rejectable behaviour. Repeatedly I have observed several common types of behaviour resulting from this belief: trying too hard, running away, or acting as if it doesn't matter. Usually this causes us to encounter the exact feeling we are most afraid of, which reinforces the belief and keeps us locked into a vicious circle.

Thousands of times I have uncovered another core belief blocking people from finding partners or allowing their relationships to work – the thought that they were not wanted by either their mother or father. This belief is quite easy to shift. Once I had healed this mistake myself, I discovered I could help others move through it in less than an hour.

I once worked with a woman whose mother had tried to abort her with darning needles. When that didn't work, she jumped off chairs and drank toxic substances. Needless to say, mother and daughter had been in power struggles since before the birth, which had made the birth experience traumatic for both of them. The mother would shout at her daughter that she hated her and had never wanted her. We started by establishing that many of the things her mother said were a result of the extreme power struggle they were both in. My client could understand this because she too said things she didn't mean in the heat of anger.

My client soon realised, with a good deal of humour, that in their war her score was far higher. She remembered with relish the dirty tricks she had successfully played on her mother, like screaming so loudly that everyone in the village knew her mother was punishing her even to the extent that at times the village priest would come running to rescue her. It was easy to take my client back intuitively to the time when the abortion attempts first began. The mother had just received word that her husband had been killed in the war. She had no money. As hard as it might be considering the truth of the circumstances, I asked my client to imagine her mother at that time as confident, resourceful and abundant. When my client had that picture, I asked her how her mother felt about her pregnancy, given she had those qualities. My client smiled and said her mother really wanted her now.

I asked my client to consider which was true, that her mother hadn't wanted her personally, or that it was pain, lack of confidence and fear that had caused her mother's actions? Obviously it had not been personal. So I asked her, now that she realised her mother wasn't personally rejecting her, if in truth she had been the one rejecting her mother all along. With a smile as big as the room, the woman admitted she had been rejecting her mother and making life hell for her. I asked her why, what was her purpose in believing she was rejected by her mother? She replied this gave her the permission to be independent and do whatever she wanted from her earliest years. (By the way, I find this is often the purpose of early trauma.) Now through her new understanding she could forgive her mother and experience a whole new level of self-worth, desirability, inclusion, fun, confidence and peace. Immediately her relationship with her mother took a giant step forward and her mother seemed completely different the next time they talked. This woman was not the most difficult client I've ever worked with in this type of trauma, but she was one of the most dramatic.

Be comforted; anyone with any willingness at all

can move successfully through deeply held beliefs like this into fulfilling and happy relationships.

Exercise

Today, consider your relationship situation.
List the beliefs you must have had for the situation to be the way it is:

_____

_____

_____

_____

If you don't like the situation or the beliefs, make a choice that will serve you better. Beliefs can easily be changed. As soon as you realise you have them, make another choice about them.
I am making new choices about the following beliefs:

_____

_____

Do You Want Your
Relationship or Your Story?

Your personality has been putting together your life story for years. Typically, it is filled with painful and heroic episodes all neatly tied together to prove what a good person you are. Anything you try hard to prove means you believe the opposite. If I were to attempt to convince you how bright I am, pretty soon you would begin to suspect that either I was insecure about my intelligence or that I was unintelligent. Our stories or concepts about ourselves are some of the most primordial aspects of ourselves that limit joy and generate all our victim patterns and problems with our families and other relationships. Let us look at some of the underlying concepts in our stories.

One way we tell our story is: 'I am the way I am because this has been done to me by others.' A more honest statement if we were truly aware of our subconscious motivation would be: 'I used others – I had them do things to me so I wouldn't have to face my fears of the next step, and so I'd have an excuse to do things my way.' That statement has been one of the fundamental dynamics in thousands of people with whom I've worked who were molested. Most of them were precocious sexually even as children. Being afraid of what they would grow into if they continued on their path of sexual precocity, they created trauma that then blocked them. That way they could satisfy their curiosity without responsibility. While not the only dynamic in molestation, this is the most common in those people with whom I've worked at a subconscious level.

Our life stories are largely composites of victim and martyr stories. Suffering is a veiled form of attack and so this is a way of feigning innocence while attacking. This is not an easy area to explore because typically we keep it all hidden from our conscious mind. Our story is all consuming. We are the heroes and heroines, but the problem is that the natural reward for all our good, or heroic actions, does not go to us: it goes to our story. It is the movie of our life.

In our movies we are the stars, the directors, producers, scriptwriters and cameramen and we make everyone else our supporting actors and actresses. But everybody else is doing the same thing. So we get into trouble in our relationships because we have been casting each other as the supporting roles in our movies. Many people script their movies as epic tragedies. It takes effort and understanding to transcend our personal stories. First we must turn our stories into happy stories, which is a great challenge for most of us. After years of working with people to clear away tens of thousands of behavioural and emotional patterns and to shift the accumulated debris of hundreds of thousands of problems, I've learned I must focus on the story that people are writing and assist them to see the payoffs they are getting are definitely not worth it.

Tragic or martyr stories can completely stop people from having a relationship or prevent a relationship going forward.

Exercise

Begin to examine your story, the one you are writing in your life, especially where it covers relationships. Take ten minutes to write at least a page about your relationship story or tell it to a friend or dictate it to a tape recorder.
My story:

_____
_____
_____
_____
_____
_____
_____
_____
_____

Pick out the key patterns which repeat again and again or which run through your story.
My key patterns are:

_____
_____
_____

What are you trying to prove by your story?

_____
_____

_____

What is the purpose of having this type of story?

_____

_____

_____

Ask yourself how many heartbreak, fear, tragedy, martyr and guilt stories you have. Ask yourself what were the results of each of these types of stories in your life and relationships? If you don't like what you've found, make some new decisions about what you want.

No matter how good your story, you deserve better.

I am turning my story over to my higher mind.

One of our great fears in life is the fear of intimacy. Intimacy is joining with someone – moving through all your blocks, considerations, and fears to a heartfelt closeness. When we get right down to the bottom line there are only two feelings, love and fear. Love is the root of very positive emotion. Love underlies joy and happiness, while fear is at the bottom of every negative emotion like anger, hatred or depression. Years ago, my wife and I discovered that our blocks and problems were in those places where we had not yet connected in intimacy. As we joined in new levels of intimacy, the problem between us and around us disappeared. We started to apply this powerful lesson to the problems of our family and friends with excellent results.

Let's consider the problem of infidelity in terms of intimacy and the subconscious mind. There are four core, subconscious dynamics that are part of the experience of infidelity as it occurs for both parties.

Fear – both parties are afraid of intimacy. The infidelity becomes a good excuse to avoid becoming more intimate, to prevent the partner meaning too much, or to end the relationship.

Power struggle – which is another form of fear.

This kind of struggle can be a method used by the 'victimised' partner to become independent, or the one having an affair to get revenge or gain control.

A lack of bonding and fulfilment which leads to fantasy, emptiness and finally infidelity.

As the result of emotional or sexual deadness, one feels desperate enough to try something, anything new.

Intimacy is love made manifest and it has the power and grace to heal all problems because one of the core aspects to any problem is that there is always separation present. For instance, when we fall ill there is a part of us that feels cut off and unloved. If we can find and integrate that part or give it love, the illness disappears. The power of intimacy and love allows a grace to manifest that transforms problems easily.

Intimacy seems to be everything we ever wanted, but we are afraid of our own sense of inadequacy and unworthiness, or we are afraid we will lose ourselves if we join with another. Intimacy is not romance, which is based on our dreams about the other; it is a real sharing of heart, mind and energy in such a way that we move forward confidently. When we are prepared to take the next step in intimacy it has the same effect as saying 'yes' to life. We move forward; we grow.

One technique which makes intimacy more possible is simply being with, or moving towards your partner without judgement, until you feel mutuality and 'joining'. When you join your partner with love, problems and their symptoms seem to disappear and a new grace and confidence appears. I have found the intimacy of 'joining' to be effective in healing. If I have a problem and my partner does not, or if my partner has a problem and I do not, or if we both have a problem, our 'joining' each other shifts the problem to a new level of experience.

As problem after problem emerges and is healed in your relationship, your enjoyment and ability to give and receive will grow. By awareness and practice you will begin to notice separation as it emerges so that you can join your partner in a new level of loving and intimacy, bringing greater success to you and to those around you.

Exercise

Today, use your present partner or, if you are single, find someone to 'join' with in order to help that person, to help yourself, or to help you both. Don't stop until you feel the release that intimacy brings. Keep moving towards them until you join them and feel joy and peace. You can do this with or without their conscious awareness, whether or not they are physically present. Practise this as often as you can, for it will empower you to move forward in your relationship whatever the nature of the problem.

I joined with:

_____

_____

I experienced:

_____

_____

I learned:

_____

_____

Having been involved in so many workshops, it is now easy for me to spot when someone is about to have a birth of love. It is like witnessing someone going through a renaissance. Their energy blossoms like spring after a long winter. They are shining and blissful and they seem to be in love with life. They are irresistible to all those around them, either in romance or in friendship.

In a long-term relationship the rebirth of love is a magnificent renewal and it does not involve just a few days of romance. It is a whole new stage of romance with revitalised sexuality. It is as if Cupid's arrow has struck you once again. Your partner finds you inspiring and falls in love with you once more. They are caught up in you, lost in the rapture of you. If this energy occurs with one person, it will occur for both, because partners can ride the energy of the rebirth.

If you are single, the energy is so electric and delectable that everyone seems to fall in love with you. Dogs, cats, men and women follow you home. Your energy can also trigger off springtime in others. It can renew your partner, your business, your out-look and your life. It can be more refreshing than a holiday and last longer. You look out at the world anew and see things as if for the first time. It gives you the freshness and openness of a beginner's mind. It takes you out of judgement and into possibility and potential. It gives you new vision and what is unessential falls away like a depleted stage of a rocket. This may or may not coincide with a change in your outside world, but it will definitely coincide with a change in your inner world. Sometimes, this seems to be something that just happens to you, like a gift from life, but it is also something you can choose to occur.

The energy of this birth is exquisite and tender. It makes you feel like singing, dancing, or writing poetry. There is a renewal of your heart and you feel closer to everyone and everything. In the same fashion, everyone feels closer to you. There is a new burst of creativity, romance, sexuality and play. This birth of love is a peak experience that can carry on for days, weeks, and even months.

Exercise

Today, give up all judgement. There is no way you could ever truly know enough about what is going on in any situation to judge it, anyone, or anything. As you give up judgement, you also give up self-attack. You then see others as needing your help rather than your judgement and attack.

Give as much as you can to everyone and everything. Invest yourself in what you do. Giving yourself is what makes anything successful. People, situations, and life will give back to you to the extent that you give yourself. This also opens you to the richness and abundance that life wants to give you. In truth, most of us are so poor at receiving that we thwart the gifts that are being offered. Give as if it was your last act on earth. Love as if it was the last time you could possibly love someone. This will give you an ability to see into people. Give it all and receive it all.

Stay in integrity. This will allow you the biggest wins. Focus on your relationships, your true love, not on someone else who has made themselves available. Temptation is one of the best ways the ego has to regain control over you and your life. The entanglements will push you into a morass of complications. Focus on true love or on your partner. They will develop the quality or the very gift with which you were tempted.

Want this new birth. Want this renewal. Ask for this new vision. Choose this expanded energy and awareness. Ask for the help of your higher mind. See it here in the present moment. Feel it here. Hear what you and friends are saying to yourself as a result of this. Ask for a miracle. Choose it to be magnificent, life-changing, and enhancing.

Sharing makes it more fun and increases the energy for everyone involved. Share this energy with everyone.

Coaching the Self Within

Coaching the self within can be an important way of balancing your life and removing it from a state of 'sacrifice'. The roles and rules that define our lives are built on the bones of old selves. Even when things look good on the surface, old negative patterns rear their heads and continue to do so, manifesting themselves as pain in the present. This situation remains until something is done to resolve it. Because we have 'forgotten' so much of our past in an effort to get away from the pain, we have also pushed away our chance to heal it through recreating understanding, bonding and love. The pain of the past has been covered over with roles and rules (compensation on our part; see page 221) and as a result, many of our gifts are buried within us. Underneath these roles and rules, under the pain and upset of the day, we have within us many wounded selves that have been emotionally arrested. We can go back and coach them. They are within us now, still waiting for help.

I have helped many people return to their childhood, to take the children they were back into their arms. They are encouraged to explain to these children that they were not at fault. It is often necessary to explain that past hurts caused by parents were not the result of neglect or even a lack of love.

In most cases, parents cause hurt to their children unintentionally, as they cope with their own fear, guilt or pain. These feelings are passed on to their children, who wrongly read them as rejection or being unloved. And it's not only small children who need to be found within ourselves. I have also supported people as they coached their adolescent selves to drop negative self-concepts that they had mistakenly picked up. They returned to certain anxious situations to give themselves advice as they began dating or experimenting with sex. In this way, they were able to reverse decisions that had led to disaster or caused them to set up patterns of self-attack or lack of self-confidence. Many people found it comforting to reassure their adolescent selves that in spite of all the spots, gawkiness, or mistaken decisions, they were going to turn out just fine.

Exercise

Here are some principles to help you coach yourself.

People act because of the way they feel. If people are acting negatively, it is because they feel that way inside.

Whatever emotional pain you suffered in a certain experience was shared by everyone else in that situation. No matter what individual circumstances caused your pain, everyone else experienced it.

What happened in the past was not your fault, but it is your responsibility! Think of that word differently: response-ability. It is your response that matters. You can change a scene, even one that took place long ago, because it is within you as an image, as a memory. Those are things that can be changed. When you do so, you will shift your present painful, unsuccessful pattern. Guilt is a trap that your ego sets to keep you from taking responsibility, and it curtails your ability to respond. Guilt keeps you from correcting mistakes, learning a lesson and making things better for yourself or anyone. Guilt is a form of self-attack that leads you to judge and attack yourself and others. Guilt keeps you from getting past an incident. It arrests your learning and maturity. Guilt becomes your excuse to hold onto a certain indulgence, however painful it may end up being.

If you do not heal your pain and guilt, you will pass it on to those you love, especially your children. You will act in such a way that this same pain or guilt is passed to them even if you are consciously struggling against it.

In this exercise, pay especially close attention to what may be holding you back from having a relationship or reaching the next step in your relationship. Go back to your childhood. Choose any specific negative instances that stand out. With the benefit of hindsight, what would you say to your earlier self? How could you bring about understanding and release yourself from that experience? Take your time. As you support a younger you, you will witness that self or selves begin to grow up. As they reach your present age, they will melt back into you, making you more confident and whole.

Go back to your adolescence and teenage years. Repeat the exercise.

Go back through your adult years, coaching and supporting yourself through any heartbreaks, disappointments or shattered dreams.

Whenever we chase a partner away, we have a blind spot that either destroys the possibility of having a relationship or mars the possibility of a joining in intimacy. Typically, this has to do with a certain style we have adopted, which is off-putting to our partner or to potential partners. It is something we either hide from ourselves, or about which we have no awareness. Most of the time we have not even noticed that our behaviour has sent others running. The first part of changing this particular issue is to find what it is that we are doing that chases people off. All too often I have heard people lament that someone has left them, only to admit that they knew exactly why they had done so. What's more, many of these people continued to behave in exactly the same way with new partners, with the same result. This type of behaviour can become subconscious, and develop into a pattern that will rear its head when we least expect it. We end up chasing away partners that we would love to have.

Many of us find that when we are single, we have an uncanny ability to push exactly the *wrong* buttons. Without consciously meaning to, we send potential partners packing. Even the most enlightened of us will have parts of our behaviour that means death to relationships. How many times have you asked yourself why you've done something that you knew would have a negative outcome? At the heart of this destructive behaviour is some form of fear – a fear of love, intimacy or sexuality. As single people, we have tests that we give potential partners. They have to pass with flying colours before we reluctantly open the doors to our hearts. What we may not realise is that the purpose of these tests is actually to flunk someone. We are, underneath it all, fearful and these tests form the reason why a relationship is not appropriate. Much of this is subconscious. We may never realise why we are unable to sustain a relationship or why potential partners always turn out to be a disappointment. The key is awareness. Without understanding or realising what we are doing, we will undoubtedly end up lonely. We chose to set up impossible standards for a reason and we need to understand just what that reason is.

I once knew an exceptionally mild-mannered young man who feigned violence when he became bored with a short-term girlfriend, knowing it was her greatest fear. Another young man spoke of his need for an ex-girlfriend while on his second date with another woman. It was their last date. I also knew someone who became overly sloppy to get rid of a potential, but fastidious partner. I have seen both husbands and wives attack their spouses just as their partners became loving, romantic and sexy. Why? Because it squelched any lucky night long before it could happen. I have witnessed histrionics, hysteria, negativity or neediness, not because there is a desire to be loved, but because there is a fear

behaviour. It keeps you unaware of what you are doing or feeling so that you continue to act in such a way.

Once you realise what you are doing, you can 'bust yourself' and honestly assess the reasons behind it. Don't beat yourself up about it. That is likely to be your normal response, but it doesn't change anything. Just apologise and make a new start. Your open sharing may be frightening to you, but it is very attractive to your partner. Even when you are sharing some unsavoury personality traits, the way in which you are doing it can be very attractive to your partner if you are open, honest and self-aware. When they have a sense of success in the relationship, they can see that things will move forward.

If you do not have a partner, share it with a friend who you know is understanding and supportive. Whatever your relationship status, it is time to commit to yourself, to your partner or to your future partner, that you will change. If you fall back into this behaviour, apologise and share what you were feeling, explaining that you acted in such a way, not as an excuse, but as a genuine communication. Then recommit to making this change.

WAY 32 Healing the Fear of the Next Step

One of the core reasons for any problem is the fear of the next step. Although we usually hide this from ourselves, we have a fantasy about what will happen if we take that step. What we usually imagine is something bad. We believe that we will find another 'bad' partner or that a trauma will repeat itself. This negative picture that we form in our minds feeds fear. I have always found fear of the next step to be unfounded. The next step, when finally taken, really frees us and moves us forward to a whole new level. When we have embraced the next step, we find the confidence we need to handle it.

Fear of the next step can stop people at many stages of their lives. In particular, it can prevent us from having a partner, or from moving on to the next step with a partner. For example, some couples are frightened to move beyond the honeymoon stage in a relationship and many relationships break up at the point when the power-struggle stage (see page 224) kicks in. Many couples are afraid to go beyond singledom to marriage. Some couples are frightened to go to the next step and have children. When a couple is frightened of going to the next step, they either try to repeat the cycle they just went through or they stay camped at the cross-roads, unwilling to go forward. This can be an extremely uncomfortable or even painful place.

When bonding (see page 221) has been lost, there is both despair and fear. Given the lack of bonding in families today, and in the world in general, it's not surprising that there is a well of sadness within each of us that manifests itself as fear in our lives. For us to reach that next step, there must be willingness, joining, forgiveness, giving, receiving, letting go or bonding in some way.

I once worked with a man whose sperm count was so low that his doctor told him he would never be able to have children. Yet, as soon as he was able to heal the trauma of his father's death, his wife was pregnant – inside a month. This man's family had refused to let him say goodbye to his father. He was just four years old, so they told him to stay outside and play. He told me that it was the last time he ever played. The trauma of being unable to say goodbye to his father effectively caused him to repudiate his childhood. This made it impossible to have children. When I took him back to his four-year-old self and allowed him to say goodbye to his father, tears of release poured down his face. When he could complete this level of the relationship with his father, he was able to understand and forgive his mother and other relatives for how they had behaved.

When you have not recovered from the pain of a past relationship – even one that has taken place in childhood – you will not allow yourself to find a new partner. The pain and loss of the past must be healed before you can successfully move on to the next stage in a relationship. Otherwise, your life stays camped at the crossroads, or you repeat the same cycle time after time, in an ever increasing spiral of dissatisfaction.

Exercise

Sometimes just the willingness to move forward is enough to allow us to do so. Today, be willing to go to the next step. Feel and imagine yourself being confident and successful at the next step. Every time you think of the future, feel good and happy about it. Set your intention to reflect the way you want it.

You can only feel fear if you believe you are alone. Imagine yourself going to the next step with God, your higher mind, or a loving partner walking beside you. Every time you think of the future, imagine this happy event. This helps to heal the old buried sense of loss we all carry within us.

In this exercise, ask your higher mind to show you through your dreams what is holding you back in relationships. Ask your higher mind to heal whatever comes to the surface and to remove the fear holding you back. Whatever has been holding you back has effectively been your excuse not to move on. With awareness you can decide what effect, if any, it has on you. You do not need to let it determine or stop your life. It can just be a lesson along the way. Your creative mind will show you how to change it from a dark lesson into one of happy learning and wisdom. You simply have to ask. It can successfully guide you through to the next stage if you let it, including bringing to you any inspiration, knowledge, or people you need to help you move forward.

WAY 33 Bonding Begins with Me

Bonding is the inter-connectedness that brings about love and success with ease. There is nothing more important than this in terms of achieving love, happiness, purpose, success, abundance, balance and meaning in life. It is such a fundamental aspect of life that in terms of success, bonding is more important than striving. Our unbonded families give rise to an unbonded society and this shows itself around the world. All of us have suffered emotional fractures which lead to our becoming weak, needy, angry, hurt, guilty, fearful, dissociated, or weighed down by burdens that we were not meant to carry. The three major roles that compensate for loss, fear, feelings of guilt, failure and separation are: sacrifice or being an 'untrue helper', dependency or neediness, and dissociation or independence.

From unbonded families come competition, fear and scarcity, fusion or loss of boundaries, difficulty and hard work. In their place there should be ease. The ego tells us that when the bonding was fractured, we murdered those from whom we separated and stole their gifts. Naturally we keep this dynamic hidden and, at least at the family level, generate and repress the shadow figures (see page 223) of the 'failure', the 'orphan', the 'thief', the 'murderer', the 'betrayer' and the 'rebel'. All of these negative self-concepts create havoc in relationships through self-hatred. Not surprisingly, it is the self-hatred that leads to self-attack, self-punishment, scarcity, difficulty, guilt, failure and valuelessness. All of these shadow figures, buried as they are at very deep levels, have major effects.

This is not the truth or the reality, but a form of ego illusion used to keep us imprisoned. Inside, we feel bad and depressed, but we hide these with our compensations. It is these family patterns that determine the patterns of our relationships. Our relationship patterns determine our patterns of failure or being a victim. All of these patterns are the opposite of bonding. Lack of bonding also manifests itself in dilemmas between career and family, or dilemmas in the choices between two partners. Loss of bonding can lead to exaggerated sexuality, sexual repression, sexual guilt and high sexual tension. This further creates casual, unbonded sex, frustration, lack of sexual attraction, or the 'Madonna-whore' syndrome, where we marry the 'good girl' or 'good boy', but go for sex with the 'bad girl' or 'bad boy'. This also means we might be wild before we get married, but good and sexually withdrawn afterwards.

The good news is that we are not 'stuck' by the effects of the past. If we stop using the past as an excuse, we can use present relationships to establish bonding once again in our lives. Lost bonding in our original families can be re-established in our present relationships, friendships and families through love, giving and forgiveness. Rebonding the family in which we grew up naturally builds a foundation of confidence, courage and communication in our present relationships. And where we have bonding our relationships are effortless and there is natural sharing and love. Even if our family was shattered, even if our family had very little bonding, we can go back and correct it. This is especially successful when we go to a root situation in the past where a level of bonding was lost and re-establish what was lost at this point.

Exercise

This exercise is great at transforming chronic pain, problems and patterns.

Exercise I
Examine the amount of bad luck, difficulty and pain you have had in your relationships. Now look back to your original family. How much bonding was there? Don't be fooled where roles such as sacrifice, dependency, nice-ness, hard work, independence, or being good or busy covered over lost bonding. What patterns can you see repeating themselves in your life now?

Work out which of these past roles you are acting out now. Imagine a friend or your partner standing in front of you and see that your role is like a suit of armour that you are wearing. Obviously it comes between you. Now relax to the point where you can visit the light inside yourself. Take as long as you need. Wait until you can see, feel, or sense this light. Now imagine it extending to your friend or partner, melting the role and its armour away until there is genuineness and connection. Enjoy this connection.

This exercise can be used to heal any bad feeling, deadness or role. All you need to do is to work out whatever is false and obstructive and visualise it between you and your partner in this exercise.

Exercise II

Go back to a scene in your family that was really painful. It is helpful to go back to a time just before a trauma begins. Once again, relax until you can sense the light inside you. Now see it extending to everyone in your family and then back and forth to each other. Once the family is reconnected with light and bonding, notice how everyone acts towards each other now.

Do this same exercise with a past relationship that was painful. You know exactly which one to work on because this person has probably come to your mind already. By doing it with this person, it will move all of your relationships forward.

Imagine your mother standing before you. From deep inside your heart and mind, open and give the gift of bonding that you brought in to save your family. See and feel yourself passing this gift to your mother until she is filled with it. Now see it going back to your grandparents and filling them. Then see it go back to your great-grandparents, filling them. Now see it going back along the whole family tree on your mother's side, helping and healing them.

Now repeat this exercise with your father and his side of the family.

Repeat exercises I and II every day this week to release yourself from the patterns of the past.

Healing the Split Mind

If you don't have a partner and you say that you want one, you are obviously suffering from a 'split mind'. If you think you want to have love in your life or success with your partner and you have neither, you are obviously suffering from a 'split mind'. When there is a conflict between what we have and what we want, we may be consciously aware of what we want, but we are unaware of our hidden, contrary feelings. In other words, part of us wants it and part of us doesn't want it. If we wanted it with our whole hearts and minds, we would have it. This is a simple principle of the mind.

We hide this part of our mind because it is less acceptable to us. Once we have hidden it, we sometimes use a person, situation, or thing to hold us back and to protect the hidden parts. This puts us into conflict, which masks the fear that is at the root of the problem. Let's take a look at the hidden part of our mind. In this part, we have a certain fantasy that something would be lost, or something fearful or negative would occur if we had what we say we wanted. Or we believe we would go into sacrifice (see page 223), we would have to do something without help, or we would have to carry someone else's load. Perhaps we fear we'd lose our freedom, lose our vivacity, lose our life as we know it.

Dwell on and become aware of your fear. What do you think the next step will do to you? What do you think might happen to overwhelm you at the next stage of partnership? Why do you have no confidence for the next stage? Do you feel adequate enough? All of our fears boil down to one basic concern: we believe that by moving on to the next step, whether it is happiness in our relationship, or just a relationship at all, we would be forced to do something. We would be forced to change. When we contemplate this, we worry that we'll be on our own, forced to do things alone, without help or support – without friends, partners or God.

Exercise

One way to build confidence when there has been conflict is to integrate the two sides of your mind. The key here is to act this out, to get in touch with the voices of both sides. Imagine all the voices that don't want a partner or the next stage with your present partner melted into one voice in one corner of the room. Go stand there and become the voice that doesn't want a partner or doesn't want the next step. Talk about everything you can think of about your fears. Speak this to the part of your mind in the opposite corner that does want a partner or the next stage with your present partner.

After you have said everything you want to say, take a step forward. Mark the place where you have stepped to with an imaginary piece of chalk. Go to the opposite corner and take up the other part of your mind, the part that does want a partner, the part that does want the next stage in your relationship. From this side, speak everything that you can think to say about how you feel, about what you want. When you're finished, take a step forward and mark this particular spot. Now go back to the other marker and become, once more, the side that is afraid to have what you want. Communicate everything you can think of, or feel like saying, from this particular spot. When you are finished, take a step forward and mark that spot. Once more cross the room to the marker for wanting true love or wanting to be closer to your partner. Now reply back to the other side, saying everything that this side can think of to say. When you finish, take the next step forward and mark that spot.

Do this until there is only one step left between the two sides. Then, from each side, speak everything you have left to say, every last little thing. Once this is completed, imagine yourself stepping forward and joining the two parts of your mind, so that they melt together. Where there were two minds, there is now one mind. Where there was conflict, feel the new confidence move through your body. Feel that the new step, whatever it is, will be a truer direction. You have now moved up to a whole new level of success. Where there is willingness there is automatically success.

WAY 35   Tantrum or Bonding

Many of us do not realise that we have a choice between tantrum and bonding. Bonding is the connection between ourselves and others and it brings about love and success with ease. This ease, intimacy and success are always sure signs that contact is made and that the connection stays. You do not have to work hard or ever to worry. You do not have to push. It is all accomplished by your intention, which sets the direction and in the bonding. Bonding brings about centredness and balance and it means there are natural levels of giving and receiving. Bonding is effortless and establishes flow, opportunity and confident anticipation.

The opposite of bonding is separation, fracturing or tantrum. When a child has a temper tantrum, it is obvious that he or she is trying to get some perceived need met. Children cry in a supermarket, throw themselves on the floor, loudly demanding things directly or indirectly through emotional blackmail. We do not realise that we have adult tantrums all the time, in the form of anger or withdrawal. Adult tantrums can take many forms, such as emotional drama, soap operas, fights or sickness. At a deeper level, all problems are a form of tantrum. Every problem at the tantrum level states: 'You didn't give me what I needed and so it is because of you that I am having this problem.' We point the finger of accusation at our parents, or at our partners or ex-partners. Of course, whenever we point the finger at them we are also pointing back at ourselves.

Suppose your parents were always fighting and ended up getting a divorce. This situation may still contain pain for you. At one level, you would be blaming your parents, at a deeper level you would be blaming yourself and at an even deeper level, you would be blaming life or even God. These tantrums become problems in relationships, where both partners tantrum, without possibly even being aware of it. In fact, for the most part, we hide the 'tantrum' side of problems from ourselves and fail to recognise them for what they are.

There are two options here: we can either continue to tantrum, or we can create new connections that allow for a partner, or a new level with a present partner. We can let go of the childhood pain, which (at the deepest level) is another excuse to tantrum for what we want. When we use this as an excuse to avoid facing our fear of love and success, we are in effect indulging ourselves. This self-indulgence will never make us happy. In fact, it is this indulgence that has prevented us from having success. It may be a tantrum that is holding us back from having a partner. The tantrum may involve experiences with an ex-partner or someone who did not treat us the way we wanted to be treated. If this is occurring, it may be a continuation of a childhood pattern of tantrums against our parents. Or our problem may be a tantrum that we are using against God, because we feel that we have been unfairly treated. Whatever the cause, tantrums guide us *away* from our life path and from our purpose. The same tantrum could be blocking a new level within a relationship. If things are going wrong, there is typically a tantrum where we are blaming someone else. The tantrum can be a way to indulge ourselves, to be independent and to behave as if we know what will make us happy. But it is definitely a place where we are not giving ourselves fully. When we give ourselves fully and give up a tantrum, we find a place of connection, contact and bonding. This is what we need for success and intimacy.

Exercise

Trust your first intuition – the first thing that pops into your mind – and ask yourself: 'If I were to know how many tantrums I have that are holding me back from having a relationship, it is probably:'

_____

_____

Or, 'If I were to know how many tantrums are holding me back right now from my partner and from a new level of relationship, it is probably:'

_____

_____

Then ask yourself: 'If I were to know what these tantrums have given me the excuse to do, it is probably:'

_____

And: 'If I were to know what these tantrums have given me the excuse not *to do, it is probably:'*

Then take a serious look at whether these tantrums and their indulgences have made you happy. If they haven't made you happy, you can choose to let the tantrums go and choose to open yourself to love, or to joining your present partner at a new level of bonding. Ask your higher mind to form a new strategy, to guide you every step of the way to open up to a new partner. Ask your higher mind to let in the grace or the gifts that would come in place of the lack of relationship, or in the place of the problem in the partnership that is holding you back from the next level of love.

Here is a quick method to heal the problem: see the problem about relationships, ask yourself who the tantrum was with, ask yourself what the tantrum is about, choose to connect in bonding with this person and let go of the tantrum.

WAY 36 Healing the Past

One of the most powerful healing concepts I have learned over the last 29 years of in-depth work is the realisation that if there is a problem, it is an unresolved problem from the past disguised as a present circumstance. Let us say that you are having a problem with your husband or men in general. You can be fairly sure that this is a pattern stemming from unfinished business with your father. Let us say there was a need that was not met by your father. You will typically try to get that need met by your boyfriend, husband, friend, or your boss. Similarly any significant fight with them will originate with your father and, if you looked deeper, a fight you are having with God. Where bonding is lost there will be fear, loss, misunderstanding and need.

The problem with any need is that we are trying to take while we cannot receive. The problem with a past need is that we are trying to get childhood needs handled in present circumstances. This is a very unsuccessful pattern and it usually compounds the original problem. Unless your boyfriend, husband, friend, or boss is operating at a high level of maturity and response, he will be put off by your neediness, which greatly lowers your attractiveness. They will also be put off by your surreptitious taking, which occurs when you are needy. You may be asking a boyfriend, husband or boss for a perfectly normal response, but your hidden attempt at taking will sabotage your own goal. Sometimes you may feel hurt that they are not giving to you and you seem to be doing all the giving. But feeling hurt is evidence that you have been *giving to take*. Your giving attempts to hide your taking. While you might deceive yourself and make it look otherwise on the surface, it always leads to the same unsuccessful and painful results.

The hurt you are feeling that is keeping you from relationships is not *just* hurt from your lost relationships, it is hurt from your childhood. The pain that keeps recurring in your present relationship is not just due to the behaviour of your partner. If you look more closely and deeply, you will notice that somehow this pain is old, unresolved pain from the past. As you move through the problem, different layers of fractures and painful feelings will come up from the past to be healed. While the problem or pain stemming from a problem is not to be trifled with, you can be grateful this past pain is coming out through this incident. When past pain is buried it clogs our mind, our heart and feelings, our success and our body. Take this opportunity and commit to healing the past as it appears in present incidences.

Exercise

Take a moment and ask who from the past has to do with your present problem in relationships? You may go through a number of people and past experiences until you get back to one of your parents. The only issues beyond this will be with yourself, or with God. All of the people who come up are in the way of your success.

Examine the present. What is the bad feeling or injustice that you feel from it? Who from your past does this have to do with? You have inherited a painful experience from them that they had inside them. With it now inside you, you will get caught in similar situations until it is healed. You will also pass on this pain or problems to those close to you. It is inevitable unless you commit to and accomplish the healing.

Here is an easy way. Go back to every person or incident until you get to your parents. What would they have needed not to have behaved as they did? Under your pain and upset, the very thing they needed is the gift you have inside yourself, waiting for this realization. Imagine yourself back at that time when the incident occurred and embrace that gift. Now imagine yourself sharing that gift with them before the negativity occurred. What do you see happening now? If it is not totally positive then there is another gift, or another layer of the same gift to give them. Repeat the exercise above until there is only peace, joy and love. Now go back to other significant relationships as they appeared and repeat this gift giving.

Examine your relationship, or lack thereof. What seems to be the issue going on that is holding you back in your life? Using your intuition, ask yourself and guess:

_____

_____

'*If I were to know where this problem began, it was
probably when I was at the age of:*'

_____

_____

'*If I were to know what was happening, it probably
occurred with:*'

_____

_____

'*If I somehow had to guess what occurred back then that
is holding me back now, it is probably:*'

_____

_____

*Imagine yourself back at that scene just before it begins to
unfold. Ask your higher mind to carry everyone involved
back to their centre, that place of peace and innocence.
If it is a major trauma you want to heal you sometimes
need to repeat this request to your higher mind and be
carried a couple of centres deeper, until you reach that
place of total peace.*

*Now imagine the light within you, the spirit within
you, extending out and connecting with everyone. Imagine everyone's light is now reconnecting with everyone
else who was there until there is a sense of joining,
bonding and everyone feels joy and peace.*

Choosing the Problem or
the Gift

Ten years ago, after about 18 years of experience as
a therapist, I noticed that one of the reasons why we
have problems is because we defend against a gift of
which we are afraid. We are afraid of this gift because
it seems overwhelming and too great for us. We are
frightened of its power and we feel somehow that
we might lose control, or that we are not capable of
the level of integrity required for such a gift. We are
afraid that we will have to come out of 'hiding' with
such a gift. Therefore, instead of the gift we choose
a problem, which is a form of control over ourselves
or over others.

Not having a partner is a problem that might hide
a gift of true love or intimacy, or it might hide
powerful gifts of sexuality or communication. The
possibilities are endless. These gifts are frightening
to the ego, so it might encourage us to choose partners that don't work, which keeps us from true love.
The ego is the principle of separation, which is the
opposite of love. The ego, or certainly a layer of it,
would be destroyed by joining. So it will suggest all
sorts of strategies that have us look for love in all the
wrong places. When we are in a relationship, the ego
suggests strategies that build up itself rather than the
relationship. Our ego wants us to be special; it wants
us to be the most important one. It is afraid that with

the next step in love, it will lose another layer of itself. It wants to control, and celebrates either domination or subjugation because it makes itself stronger. It is afraid of equality, intimacy and joining.

I have found that helping people find the gifts hidden under their problems is one of the easiest ways to collapse major problems. If a person can realise or even guess what gift they have and then embrace it, the problem (which was a defence to hide or block the gift) falls away. It is best to use your intuition here because when we use our thinking mind, it is a sure sign we are blocking our gift. Most thinking, unless it is meditative or creative, is dictated by the ego.

Exercise

Whether you have a partner or whether you're looking for a partner, it takes some time to recognise the problem that is in the way. What negative emotion seems to be in the way? What unmet need seems to hold you back? Now imagine that these needs, feelings and problems are a defence against a gift. Take some time and dwell on what that gift could be. What is it that could have been hidden away? A gift is not for us alone – it is something that we give to ourselves and to everyone around us. It makes us all feel good and it adds to our lives. Our higher mind is willing to be in charge of this particular gift, to show us the right and natural way to use it. It keeps us in integrity rather than using it to indulge ourselves, or to prove that we are more special. It adds to our responsiveness. *Our higher mind will help us use the gift most effectively, to guide and educate us about this gift, enhancing it for everyone's benefit.*

As you dwell on what this gift could be, allow it to come to your mind. What could this particular problem be a defence against? What is it that is so good that we are trying to hide from ourselves? What can we now willingly open up and embrace? Sometimes a problem is exactly the opposite to the gift. For example, the problem of having no partner could mask a gift of true love. As you embrace this gift, feel the energy of it filling you. If you have a partner, feel yourself sharing it with them. If you have yet to find a partner, feel yourself sharing it with your true love to come. If you find you have closed off your intuition, ask your higher mind to show you what the gift is within the next 24 hours. Just before you go to sleep you can ask to see it in your dreams and recognise it as your gift. Ask that your gift shows itself so powerfully and dramatically that you will know it and be able to share it for your own happiness and for that of the people around you.

WAY 38 Giving Up Grievances

All of our problems stem from our grievances in some way. Feelings of exhaustion, painful emotions, poor physical health or money problems are all symptoms of grievances. Where we don't have love in our lives we have a grievance against someone. We may have felt hurt or used by someone, so we blame them, or hold a grievance against them. Maybe the grievance is against our parents, maybe it is against life or God, or maybe it's against ourselves. All of these grievances serve to stop us and at least one part of our lives becomes arrested. This is obvious because we either do not have a partner, or we are stuck in a relationship that is uncomfortable and not moving forward.

Now is our opportunity to ask ourselves who these grievances are against. If we begin with the family we grew up in, we can ask ourselves these questions: What grievances do we have that are keeping us from a relationship or keeping our relationship from moving forward? Who in our present and past relationships do we have a grievance against, that may be stopping us from moving forward now? Do we have a grievance with ourselves? What are the grievances with our significant other or our last significant other? What are our grievances with life or God?

If we explore these grievances deeply, we will find that they are places where we feel guilty, where we feel as if we were to blame. We cover over our guilt with blame and tend to project onto others the guilt that we have about ourselves. Our willingness to forgive ourselves and others is what allows us to move on. We could choose to have the grievances that block us or we can have creativity, love, vision and the ability to receive. Do we want to forgive the grievance and let it go so that our life might move forward? Or do we want the problem that a grievance always generates? When we finally forgive, we can see that the grievance was a mistake. We come to a new understanding, and things are finally complete. A lesson has been learned and a mistake corrected. When we forgive we help others, we help ourselves and we clear this area of hidden guilt, which allows us to open to the next step and move through the fear that being stuck in guilt hides.

Our grievances serve to protect our hidden fears. If we are willing to be courageous, if we are willing to have our true partner, if we are willing to move forward with our present partner, we can make the choice to forgive. Otherwise our grievances become the excuse not to move forward.

Exercise

Ask your higher mind to be in charge of the forgiveness. Ask that it is done easily, gracefully and smoothly, and that you can now move forward. Ask that you do not use this grievance to hold yourself back. It is time to move forward and begin to live again. When we have a grievance, we head towards more pain, failure, illness and death, instead of towards love and success.

You do not deserve this problem. You deserve true love. Forgiveness will be the way out. Otherwise, you will not escape your own judgement and attack on others. If you are not in a relationship, examine the problem with your last partner. If you are now in a partnership, take a close look at the problem now. Examine the grievance that you must have underneath to keep such a problem going. Isn't it possible that the grievance you have is something you may be doing? In other words, if you have a grievance with someone else, it may actually reflect something that you actually believe about yourself. Something deep within you is reflecting on another person. You may be terribly frightened by the idea that you could be like this and as a result, you may be compensating greatly. You would probably rather die than believe that you are capable of doing such a thing or behaving in such a way.

If you have a strong reaction to the very thought that the grievance you hold with someone else may actually be a reflection of something from within you, it is a fairly sure sign you have a bad case of compensation (see page 221). It's important to remember that at a fundamental level, whatever you believe about someone else, you believe about yourself. This belief may have stemmed from something that happened a long time ago. It simply became buried and you have compensated for it. Begin to explore how you might be deceiving yourself, how you might be holding yourself back by such a belief. Consider all the wasted time, energy and sacrifice you have put *into proving that you are not the way this person is. This quality is not there in this person by accident. It is there to help you forgive so your hidden guilt is released and the relationship moves forward.*

It is time to let go of your grievances and embrace life. Embrace true love, or the new level of true love that is coming to you. There cannot be scarcity or problems in love unless you are investing yourself in grievances. It's time to let those go and enjoy what now wants to come to you, at a whole new level of relationship.

Love always beckons, invites and welcomes. It always includes, always extends and joins. Your ego, on the other hand, wants to be right; it wants to win. Holding grievances is effectively the ego's plan for your happiness. It encourages you to feel that you are better than someone else and to see yourself as innocent or injured as a result of their actions. The ego is afraid of love. The ego has no place for love; it is the principle of separation, made up of fear, guilt, competition, holding on, revenge and righteousness. It feels inadequate in the face of love, so it wants to dominate, or be dominated, rather than be equal in the intimacy of love.

As soon as you judge a person you begin to feel bad yourself, so how could grievances lead to happiness? Your grievances state: 'I am not responsible for my life or my experience. They did this to me.' This is a place of weakness and immaturity, which is unattractive and tends to keep us in the victim/victimiser cycle. It says: 'I will be happy if someone else or something else changes'. We then decide who or what needs to change and when they do not, we judge them and 'dole out' grievances. But only if we change and grow in maturity and love will the situation empower others to change. If we do not change, the situation will not change. To find your beloved or to change the situation with your present partner so that they become your beloved again, you must first be willing to change. Otherwise, you will alternate between grievances with the present or past partner as you fantasise or search for someone better. You will never find the perfect partner until you are the perfect partner.

Typically in a relationship, one partner is at the same level of maturity as the other, or the relationship will deteriorate and end quickly. Unless, of course, one partner is using the other to hold themselves back. We are usually blind to our own immaturity, but view our partner's immaturity as being glaringly obvious. We pretend that we are not choosing for them to act as they are, so that we can indulge ourselves or have an excuse to do as we please. Therefore, we feel justified in our grievances and will often try to convince everyone around us how wrong our partner is, or how wrong men or women are in general. In this way we hide our need to change. It is our change that will work to improve our situation.

When we have been victimised, we become blind to our victimisation of others. This can come from demands, expectations, needs, complaints, control or independence – anything that keeps us from intimacy and equality. It is only where we heal the victim within us that we have the compassion, confidence, strength, wisdom, responsiveness and authority to help someone else heal the victim inside them. It is only when we commit to intimacy and equality that we can have partnership.

Exercise

It is time to examine your past grievances in significant relationships. What was the grievance? What did you demand for them to change? What change did you need to make in that situation? Are you willing to make that change now? If you are, commit to that change in yourself. Anything that is holding you back emotionally may begin to come up. As it does, simply make the commitment for the change again. This is one of the easiest ways to create change. Each commitment will bring the change closer until it is present.

Another way to bring about a change is to forgive yourself. You will notice that when you have fully forgiven yourself, there will be nothing for which to forgive others. What change are you being asked to make now that could vastly improve your relationship situation? Sit quietly with your eyes closed for 10 to 15 minutes. Ask your higher mind to show you the way. At the end of your quiet time, ask your higher mind to make any necessary changes and inspire you where you need to act.

WAY 40   Unlucky in Love

We feel unlucky in love when we keep making bad choices in our relationships, or when we have no relationship at all. Most people do not realise that at some level we all make our own luck. We must allow for it and then give ourselves permission to have it. This begins by not being frightened of luck and success. We must let go of our great unconscious fears, such as the fear of having it all, of being that great or succeeding that much. We get lucky because we feel innocent, worthy of winning and in the flow. Being lucky is also being carefree, rather than being careful or careless. It means moving beyond the fear that would lock us into being careful or the reaction and denial against our fear that would lead to carelessness. Guilt is another killer of luck. Roles and sacrifice, which hide our guilt, but not our emotional heaviness or unworthiness, lead to our being careful so we do not fail. Even if we succeed, we can become worn and tired. On the other hand, being careless goes beyond mere inadvertence, or accidents. Carelessness can actually lead you into the martyr role, or it can be a reaction against the heaviness and sacrifice of other roles. This reaction can lead to dissociated independence, or even wildness, but still the same problems of role-playing (see WAY 20) and guilt remain underneath. On the surface this leads to plain bad luck.

Luck comes from being in the flow, with all the naturalness, spontaneity and lack of self-consciousness involved. It comes from the suspension of thinking, which makes us self-conscious and takes us out of the flow. Every one of the thousands of personalities inside us has an idea of what would make us happy and gives us a myriad of jobs to do so that we can reach our goal. Each personality inside has its own logic system and makes us watch ourselves whenever we do something. Have you ever tried to watch yourself when you walked? Being self-conscious is like having a camera on you all the time. Being self-conscious means that we hear all the voices inside commenting and criticising our every act. All of this stops the flow and stops the luck. Luck is not self-conscious but instinctive. The more the mind is turned off, or focused by concentration, the more inspired our action. This allows us to be in tune with how things are unfolding so that we act boldly and smoothly.

Being unlucky in love means that at some level we did not get over an event from the past. It says that we feel we are a victim of love, or that we are a victim because we don't have it. Being unlucky is giving a message to some significant person in your life, saying: 'I am partner-less because of you. I lack confidence because you never showed me how, or because of what you did to me.' What we do not realise is that under the painful guise of being a victim there is an attempt to prove that someone else did something wrong and it harmed us. At times we are willing to hold up our whole lives, just to prove that someone did us wrong. We use our bad luck as an attempt not only to defeat them, but also to defeat ourselves and even God. All of the times when we have been victimised give us an excuse not to have to face our fear and move forward. They give us a chance to keep control of some situation. Sometimes we are trying to control ourselves, because we are afraid we would be too wild, or too sexual, or too great, if we did not have something to use to keep ourselves under control. Maybe we are using our victimisation to control others, or our partner, in order to have things our way. It's a way of avoiding facing certain fears. At times, people also use victimisation to prevent themselves from having a partner. In the end, this all spells bad luck.

It is important to understand that the feelings we experienced when we were victimised are the same feelings experienced by the victimiser, though they are totally repressed. We can either free ourselves, or we can keep passing on the wound to others. The parts of us that are wounded are literally different selves within us and they have been unable to evolve, or move forward, since they were wounded. These selves contain the pain of the past and lack the maturity of our present self. The needs and fear left over from this event surface from time to time, setting up scenes of dependency and unattractiveness – or even independence as a compensation to hide these feelings. In independence, we then tend to draw people toward us with the same wounds, needs and fear. But because we are in denial over our own pain, we will ride roughshod over others' pain, needs and fears, inadvertently bringing up their old wounds. We usually run from their needs because we are afraid of our needs. We cannot see that these people and situations are brought to us to heal the past and ourselves. If we choose the healing, we will find we have the confidence to go forward once again. If we choose luck, we will begin to find the flow of opportunities beginning once again. Somehow, we will feel that life is opening up all around us. We will get out of the place where we feel unlucky in love and irresistibility will return. If we are in a relationship, we will find that the next level of true love with our partner is much more important than past victim agendas and things will begin to move our way. We do not need the control we get by having difficulty. We can trust the flow. We can embrace our luck in our relationship and in our life.

It is time to re-examine and release all these places where we believed we were a victim. We can keep using the times when we were harmed as a way of attacking others, but it will not make us happy. We can keep using the past as an excuse not to move forward, or we can free ourselves and just decide to grow past this. Someone who is lucky lets go easily to be in the flow. Being lucky in love and having true love is so much more worthwhile than living in the past and fighting old battles, especially when the past is used as a way of hiding and avoiding

the present. As we go forward, everyone succeeds. As
we get lucky, we give everyone permission to get lucky.

Exercise

Choice. Letting Go. Asking for Help

*If you are frightened of being successful, ask yourself:
'Why?' 'Who does this have to do with?' 'Why am I
afraid to succeed now?' You can go back to the situation
and make a choice for true love; you can make a choice
to heal this pattern. Is this aspect of trying to prove it
is someone else's fault more important to you than true
love? Is what you are trying to prove about yourself,
about life, about relationships, about men or women,
more important to you than being lucky or having true
love? Is being right more important to you than being
lucky or having true love or happiness? Is having control
what you really want? Will this really make you happy
to have things your way? Has your strategy for true
love ever really worked for your business? Would you
be willing to let go of this control that comes from being
a victim?*

*It is time to make a new choice. Do you want to be
lucky in love? Are you willing to stop trying to defeat
others? Can you accept that every time you defeat others,
you defeat yourself? Are you willing to let go of all this
proving and being right? Because what you prove, you
really do not believe and where you have been trying
to prove yourself right, you have actually felt wrong or
guilty inside. Would you give up the revenge of being
a victim for the gift of luck? Would you be willing to*

*regain your power and attractiveness in love by letting
go of attachment from the past? At any point that you
feel you don't have confidence, you can ask your higher
mind to restore it to you and show you the way forward.
You do not have to rely on yourself. You have probably
learned by now that the ego is always unlucky in love.*

Choose your luck. Embrace your luck in love!

Healing Your Wounded Selves. Integration

*Go back to a scene where you were emotionally wounded.
Ask yourself this question: 'If I were to know how many
selves were wounded, there were:'*

_____

_____

*Imagine yourself back in the original scene. Look
inside the one who wounded you. Notice that they
have all the wounded selves inside them that caused
them to wound you. Imagine all the wounded selves
in you going up and embracing all the wounded selves
in them, just holding them. Soon, both your selves and
their selves will begin growing up until they reach your
present age. They will then melt into you, reconnecting
the wires that were cut in your mind and heart when
you were emotionally wounded. This new energy will
certainly add spirit to your lives. Do the above exercise
with the different painful scenes in your life once a day
for the next week.*

*Every night and every morning choose the flow.
Choose luck. Choose miracles!*

WAY 41 Healing the Mistake of Sacrifice

Fear of sacrifice is one of the big issues that frightens people away from relationships and causes endless amounts of trouble within relationships. Sacrifice is a form of counterfeit giving and loving that the ego employs to keep separation, fear, competition and deadness on-going. Giving and receiving are inextricable, but sacrifice gives and never receives. It lies in wait to 'take' later.

Sacrifice is a compensation for feelings of guilt, failure and valuelessness. We give to prove that we are good or deserving. Because our giving isn't genuine – because we are trying to prove something in which we do not believe – we will never reap any rewards. Sacrifice is not true genuine giving because it hides surreptitious taking. In sacrifice, there is a belief that 'you are better than me, so if I sacrifice myself, we can both use your identity to carry us'; or, 'I will lose now in sacrifice but you have to lose later when it is more important.' This is a competition based on scarcity (see page 223).

The belief that someone has to sacrifice pervades relationships. Sacrifice can also be a way of using someone else to hold ourselves back. When you hear someone claim that a person used them, you can bet their hidden agenda was to use the other to hold themselves back. When a person has enough fear of sacrifice, it will keep them away from relationships. Many independent people realise that while they are tough and independent on the outside, they are really marshmallows on the inside. They realise that they have a tendency to give away too much when they fall in love, so they stay careful, in control and as independent as possible.

In most families the loss of bonding automatically sets up traps of sacrifice, lost boundaries (fusion; see page 221), and dissociated independence that can last a lifetime. Our family dynamics, for the most part, are set up by the ego as a conspiracy – a trap so good it looks like we will never get out of it. It does this by turning the need to help and save our family into an impossible task. The perceived impossibility of saving our families has become so strong and prevalent that the common belief of therapy today is 'Don't try to save your family!' The problem with this is that we are all compelled to try to save our families. It is a built-in need. Our lack of success leads to guilt, failure, valuelessness, fusion, loss of boundaries, co-dependency, sacrifice, roles, other compensations and, finally, burn-out.

It is not surprising that we become very independent from our families, either acting as if we don't care, or moving as far as possible away from them. Many therapists today suggest that people remain independent so as not to lose their boundaries. But this merely hides the lost bonding and keeps the client locked in one of the main roles of independence. Independence is compensation for old wounds and sacrifice. It is dissociation parading as freedom. The pattern and potential of our life's purpose is tied in with healing and helping the family. Our family and its issues demonstrate the challenges our soul has set for itself to heal and to learn. Our family gives us a blueprint for our potential and our purpose. Our family patterns are at the heart of all our life patterns. Our family patterns lead to our relationship patterns and our relationship patterns lead to our victim or success patterns. Our childhood reflects our whole soul pattern in both its giftedness, and what we have come to heal.

Families are second only to our own relationships in their importance in our lives. The family conspiracy is used so widely and successfully by the ego that in all of my world travels, I have met possibly one person who grew up in a bonded family. Since she was interviewing me on the phone from London to Taiwan, it was not actually something I could verify. A bonded family is a happy, supportive, co-operative, successful, and loving family. An unbonded family is a family where we are in sacrifice to some degree or another, playing roles in an attempt to save the family. Some people act out independent roles or even seem lost from the family, while others, who play dependent roles almost continuously, need help. The family is so crucial to us that we are willing to get into trouble, stay invisible, leave the family itself, give up our health, our sexual integrity and even our lives in an effort to save the family. These are all roles and none of them is effective.

This sacrifice of the past scares many people

away from relationships because we feel that it is impossible to have a life of our own if we have a relationship or family. We believe that it is not possible to have a life after commitment. This scares many people into staying independent. Yet the sacrifice and fusion, loss of boundaries and co-dependence are in all of us, whether we stay independent or not. As a matter of fact, the extent of our independence is the extent to which we are compensating for the sacrifice or loss of boundaries inside us. This sacrifice and its incumbent deadness is so strong that we spend a whole stage in relationships learning to heal it.

The counterfeit joining of sacrifice is a fusion or confusion of individual boundaries that creates deadness, both emotionally and sexually. This 'dead zone' comes after the power struggle in our relationships. This confusion is the ego's best attempt to sabotage 'joining', one of the key healing principles of power struggle. We all must go through this stage and learn to heal sacrifice and fusion so we can reach bonding and the partnership stage in relationship. We cannot even have a relationship, much less a successful relationship, until we first get through the fear of sacrifice and finally through sacrifice itself.

Exercise

If you are not in a relationship, commit to getting through this fear of sacrifice. Choose that you will give yourself fully, rather than sacrifice, which involves working hard while withholding yourself.

Commit to your partner as if you were choosing them for the first time. This can move you through hundreds and sometimes thousands of steps or lessons about sacrifice.

Ask your higher mind to clear this sacrifice or its fear for you. Know that the next step and its incumbent sacrifice can come up within seconds of having it cleared, especially if you are working through 'dead zone' issues. Be aware of this and when it comes up just ask for help once again. If you are not aware of the clearing and the few seconds of relief before the next layer of heaviness hits, you think nothing happened or that things got worse. Just keep asking.

Ask for the truth to come to you. This is a way to clear the trap and illusion of sacrifice. Desire and want the truth with your whole heart. It will free you and the situation.

Temptations – Accept
No Substitute

For a number of years I have noticed women coming
to my seminars hoping to find a partner. Often
they blossomed in joy, but the next time I visited
their country they were dejected and depleted once
more. Some time ago I decided to take a closer look
at what was going on. I found out that they had
found the perfect mate within a fortnight, except
for one thing – he was married or in another relationship. Was it coincidence, or bad karma, or was
something else afoot? Within six months I had the
answer.

When you are wide open in joy, your ego doesn't
have much to stop you with, so it offers you a last
trap. Along comes a *simulated* Mr or Ms 100 per
cent perfect. They are really Mr or Ms 85 per cent
perfect because they are in another relationship.
But, because he or she has not had someone to
love and be loved by for a long time, the temptation is seemingly irresistible and they fall into the
trap of a triangular relationship. This is a horrible
trap which causes guilt and delays happiness. The
usual scenario is that the person who is wide open
chooses Mr or Ms 85 per cent and completely misses
Mr or Ms 100 per cent because they are deeply
involved in the triangular relationship. Sometimes

they notice the 100 per cent possibilities but miss their importance because they are already lured into the trap. Now when I see women leaving a workshop in that starry-eyed way I give them my best advice: if they meet Mr 85 per cent, enjoy the connection and friendship, but don't get involved romantically because Mr 100 per cent is waiting in the wings, he's on his way. It is important not to settle for less. If they follow my advice, they will have a new friend and very soon a true love. Don't settle for less.

Just as you are about to have a whole new level of romance with your partner, just as they are about to develop a gift you always wanted them to have, your ego tempts you with someone outside your relationship. Your ego does this to preserve itself, leading you down the rosy path of temptation and promising new levels of success and intimacy. Once you are embroiled in a triangle relationship, all kinds of feelings of guilt and failure emerge, some of which stem from childhood. This happens because we are so tempted by this particular quality and we cannot believe our partner could have it. Yet, if we recognise the quality that tempts us, and realise that this very same thing is about to develop with our partner, we can bring this 'temptation energy' home to our partner. Once this energy is invested in our partner, they develop the quality we were tempted by and we go into a new level of romance. This can happen in just a few weeks. Keeping the form of our existing relationship, but staying caught in the fantasy of the temptation, blocks the new stage about to develop in our relationship.

Accept no substitute! Everyone wins more if you

do. Stay open to having it all. It's what you deserve and what you have come to share with a true partner.

Exercise

Today, affirm you can have a 100 per cent relationship with your partner or if you are single with someone who is totally free. Enjoy your new connections.

Trust yourself and trust the process.

If you stand empty handed with trust and joy, your attractiveness only grows. If a Mr or Ms 85 per cent shows up, it's usually an indication that Mr or Ms 100 per cent is close behind.

I can have my 100 per cent perfect relationship.

WAY 43 Depression

Named by the World Health Organisation as the number-one health problem in the world, depression can lead to many specific symptoms and diseases. One of the things that depression does is block an opening to true love. It blocks you from being able to find your beloved and it blocks you from going to the next level with your beloved, because you are both too tired and feel too unattractive to go forward. Our ability to compensate for pain and problems is so developed that we can hide our depression and go on for decades as if they are not there. But sooner or later they will surface as issues, symptoms, or problems that have to be dealt with. In relationships they can create invisible walls.

Depression comes from a loss of a person, a situation or an event from which we have not recovered. Depression can also result from the loss of a cherished dream so shattering that we have never regained our energy, our hope and our willingness to begin again. Sometimes we compensate for this depression by pushing ourselves, being very busy, or by doing as much as we can, acting cheerfully, when underneath there is still a fetid lake of depression. Because we have not recovered from these old losses, a depression can take the form of attachment, of holding on to that lost person or dream. Therefore, our ability to have a new relationship or go to the next level is already filled by this attachment. Depression only allows for relationships that do not work or are bad for us – if it allows for any relationship at all. As they resurface, depressions can also lead to a dependency on drugs or alcohol, or we can become just plain needy in general as we seek to fill the gap left by the shattered dream.

When we have a partner, an old loss can keep us from moving forward because, as we begin to move toward our partner, dire negative emotions or lethargy may begin to surface. These emotions may include pain, feelings of loss and hopelessness. Rather than face these feelings, we withdraw again from our partner. We withdraw rather than stepping forward through these painful emotions to experience a new level of connection with our partner.

To heal the depression, we can imaginatively return to the place of the shattered dream or broken heart, and feel what the child within us was feeling when the depression began. The old depression may be something left over from our childhood. It may come from an illness, the loss of a family member, the shattering of a family, the divorce of our parents, taking on the depression of one of our parents through fusion (see page 221), or inheriting a depression from one or both sides of our families. We might have hidden the depression for many years, but there were other side-effects. Sometimes it was so painful that the child within us died or went into a coma. Sometimes the pain was so great that we lost not only that 'self,' but the others that took its place. Sometimes the child within was wounded and became emotionally crippled, or emotionally arrested at that age.

When this occurs, the mind creates other selves to take their place. If we can imaginatively go back to those situations, find those wounded children, and love them until they begin growing again, they will grow to our present age, and then re-integrate or melt them back into us, reconnecting those wires in our mind and heart that were cut. The key is to use our intuition to find these parts of us. If we find lost selves, we can breathe life back into them so that they awaken once again. This has the effect of ending conflicts and depression and bringing about new levels of confidence, success and ease. It transforms negative emotion into willingness to go forward in happiness. Recovering these pieces re-energises us and gives us a new outlook on life.

Once recognised, depression can be healed in many ways. We can have the courage to embrace the negative emotions, to wade into the soup of fear, anger and hurt and to feel the loss of that person, that dream, or that situation. We must feel all of these feelings until they are gone and then feel through the fear of the next step, the fear of giving up the control that the depression gives us before we can move on. As we experience all of these feelings rather than hiding and dissociating from them, each one will gradually melt away. Sometimes experiencing these feelings until they are gone can be completely exhausting and leave us enervated by these old feelings as they emerge. But as we feel them aggressively, leaning into them as much as we can, so that we feel every sensation, we will gradually regain our energy and motivation. As we accelerate our emotional 'burn', we learn gradually not to be frightened of our feelings. The listless cloud of enervation that our life has been under melts away. As we experience the painful feelings, we reconnect with our heart, we win back parts of us that we threw away or disallowed and then we find new gifts buried under the depression. To complete this process is to find buoyancy, a new lease on life, and a feeling of springtime.

In a relationship, we can join with our partner to get through all of this pain. We simply imagine ourselves emotionally stepping through each painful feeling. As we make our partner more important than this old pain, we will finally step through the separation caused by the fear of our buried feelings and join them. When we value making our heart one with their heart and our mind one with their mind, we can move through dire feelings of loss, shattered dreams, guilt, fear, failure, valuelessness and even death temptation with relative ease and efficiency. In rare circumstances, instead of finding joy when we join our partner, a whole new repressed issue from an unconscious level can burst forth. We will know if it is from an unconscious level because we will be on our knees with pain. In this case, we just repeat the exercise and join with our partner, valuing them more than the pain. We will then have succeeded in clearing two big levels.

Exercise

Imagine yourself floating back in time and space until you reach your biggest depression, or until you reach your last depression. Who was there with you? What was going on? What was happening to cause this feeling of depression? You can use the ways already mentioned (re-integrating our wounded selves, 'burning' your emotions, or joining your partner) to heal this depression. Choose the method that you instinctively think is right.

Think of everyone in that past situation and realise that they were also feeling that depression or the emotions that lead to feeling depressed. Typically, someone else's behaviour led to that depression. Realise that the cause of their behaviour was that same loss and depression. Without this, they would not have acted in a way that caused you to experience such loss. What has happened is that you have taken on their depression and it has become a part of your life. Underneath this depression, there still exists the gift that you brought in to help them heal their depression. Imagine yourself back at that time and place and imagine it is before the incident occurred. Now imagine that within you is the very gift that you would need to share with them to heal their depression.
Ask yourself the following questions:
'If I were to know, what is that gift?'

_____

_____

'What is it that would help them to heal themselves?'

_____

_____

Imagine yourself opening up your mind and heart and giving that gift. Remember the alternative to realising and giving your gift is receiving their depression and passing it on. You can heal this pattern for them, yourself and anyone involved. Either the loss will keep breeding or the healing will now occur. This gift giving is one of the easiest ways to move through the deepest patterns of guilt and depression. You brought this gift to help someone through this particular situation and to save them from this particular depression. So imagine yourself energetically giving this gift to all the people in that situation, mind-to-mind, heart-to-heart and soul-to-soul. As you share this gift with them, how are they now acting? Notice that how they acted before was a cry for help, specifically a cry for your help. You can help them by sharing this gift to free them and yourself from this pattern that you have taken on. By healing this pattern now, you will have this gift as a part of your being to share with people to help them through their problems and depressions.

Sometimes a part of the depression will clear up, but other parts remain. This just means there is another gift or another layer of the same gift to be shared or another incident to be healed. As you share these gifts and heal these depressions, layer by layer, those you love or were called upon to help are freed. You then are also freed. Once this is accomplished, you can have the renewal and springtime that such a breakthrough brings.

WAY 44 The Hidden Agenda

Let us travel once more into the subconscious mind. When there is a difference between what we say we want and what we have, then we are in conflict. If we were not in conflict, we would have what we want, such as true love, or a happy relationship with our partner. When we don't have what we want, there is something more important to us that is keeping us from having true love or peace in our present relationship.

The subconscious principle that I have seen proven true over and over again is that what we want is what we have. If what a person has is different than what they want, they have a hidden agenda and are in conflict inside themselves. Naturally, the part we have kept conscious is what we thought we wanted and we have buried the rest. Let me give an example. Recently I asked a woman, who was very aware of what she wanted in a relationship, to tell me the first thing that popped into her mind as I asked her questions. I asked her what she wanted in relationships about fifty times. All kinds of things came out and she was astounded and shocked by her response. For the first half a dozen times what popped into her head were things like true love, happiness, joy, romance, peace, etc. As we continued other goals started creeping in – things like control, pain, anger, attack, self-attack and domination. As she went on, she began alternating between positive and negative goals, including things like death, revenge, unhappiness, drama and slavery. This was so unlike this woman – as she appeared on the surface – that it surprised all of us. She appeared to be an aware, deep, sweet, fun-loving person full of positive hidden aspects, coupled with a generally loving, comforting personality. Yet the conflict that came out of her mouth is shared by so many other people with whom I have repeated this exercise.

The principle at work here is that when you do not have something you think you want, you are afraid of it. Most of the time we hide these conflicts from ourselves and go naively along thinking that we know what we want. If we continue to think this way, there will be a lot that we will never know about ourselves, a lot that we remained frightened about and a lot that we never have in life and relationships. On the other hand, if we are willing to explore what we have pushed into darkness we can begin to change, make new decisions and choose not to be the victim of our circumstances. Examining what we have denied and hidden is the first step in healing.

Exercise

This exercise can be the beginning of freedom. You must be willing to venture past your conscious mind, which is just supporting the ego's status quo. Trust your intuition and believe in whatever pops into your mind.

*Depending on whether you want to have a relationship
or are already in a relationship, say to yourself:
'In the situation regarding relationships, what I want to
happen is:'*

_____

_____

*Or: 'In the situation regarding my present relationship,
what I want to happen is:'*

_____

_____

*Repeat whatever question is appropriate for you and keep
asking the same question for the next three minutes. This
is a very good exercise to do with someone else, who can
ask you the questions and write down your answers. Or
you can tape-record the questions at regular intervals and
play them back for yourself, hitting the record button to
answer.*

*If you have been willing to get out of your conscious
mind you will find that your answers point towards many
conflicting goals. These goals come from different parts of
your mind, or different personalities, all of which think that
different things will make them happy. The personalities
that want negative things are usually arrested parts of
you that were stopped in their growth through painful or
traumatic incidents. They typically come from the same
situations that brought about the many conflicted goals.
You can resolve these conflicted parts easily if you are
ready to be finished with your fear, and be successful in
a future relationship, or the one in which you are now.*

Simply choose that all of these goals or personalities

be integrated. I could write down 50 different integration exercises here. However, the essence of all of them is to choose that these parts, going in opposite directions and wanting different things, be joined. In integration what is negative falls away and the energy is used for a positive goal. A new level of wholeness and confidence emerges because you have achieved a new level of integrity by your awareness and integration. If you still feel too frightened to choose integration, ask your higher mind to take care of the fear that is holding you back. You can choose or ask your higher mind to integrate all of these conflicting parts. By moving through these conflicts, you resolve everything that holds you back from true love.

WAY 45 Healing Projection

Over the years, I have heard groups of women (and individual men) complain, sometimes bitterly, about the opposite sex. Many times it was easy to see that they were portraying the very characteristics that they had been complaining about. This would have been funny if they were not in such pain. Once you realise how profound the concept of projection is, you realise that people only ever complain about themselves. The old sayings best sum up projection in its simplest terms: 'It takes one to know one', or the one about 'the pot calling the kettle black'. Projection comes from rejecting some quality about ourselves, burying it and denying that it is there. And because we can not stand the fear and or guilt surrounding this quality, we project it out on some person or situation around us. We even do this with gifts of which we are frightened. We judge, repress and deny them and then project them out on someone outside us. Of course, whatever we have projected outside us does not clear the conflict within us. It just brings us into conflict with those people or things outside us.

Where we have projected a negative quality, we will see others as deserving judgement, attack and punishment. If we didn't feel guilt we could have no judgement and we would just see that others outside us need our assistance. Projection is a powerful mechanism in our mind. It literally peoples the world and writes the scenarios surrounding us. We do this in consensus with everyone else's projections. So we can get a hundred people to agree with us about a certain person or situation, but if we were armed with healing, or truth, we could actually change all of this perception by changing our perception. I have seen this occur hundreds of times. It is powerful healing. Learning how to use this principle is one of the great gifts of self-empowerment.

Your perception shows you your projection. At the deepest level, the family with which we grew up and our family or partner now, are the best mirrors to show us the negative parts of our souls that we have come to heal. It also shows what gifts are there for us to enjoy. The ability to transform our negative perceptions of others close to us is tied in with our soul purpose. The more we accomplish the healing, integration, or forgiveness, which is part of our soul's purpose, the more the negative qualities disappear in those close to us and we are empowered to be gifted, attractive and open to true love. Simply put, if some quality upsets us, rather than touches our compassion, we have a negative self-concept in that very area. When we project that negative self-concept outside us, we will typically use one of two different styles or bits of both. One style is that we realise we do the same thing and the other style is that while we believe we are like that ourselves, we compensate or act in an opposite manner. For instance, if we have projected out the quality of 'stinginess' on our partner, we might notice that at times we are also stingy. Or in the case of the second style, we feel we would rather die than be stingy. This reaction is a sure sign of compensating behaviour. This compensating style means we will be acting generously, but without the reward or receiving which naturally comes from giving. We might momentarily feel good, but most of the reward goes to attempting to prove that we are not stingy.

Once we realise the part that the projection factor plays in relationship, we also realise that it is a key concept that can be used either for healing or for complaints in a relationship. It literally means that all of our relationships are made up of and reflect, our relationship with ourselves. This radical idea gives us a key principle to transform what is around us, especially our relationships. By changing our mind, we can transform our relationship with ourselves. To change the world around us, or to change the life in our partner rather than the partner in our life, we must first realise that we have been projecting onto others. Once we recognise the very nature of perception as projection and further recognise the style that we have been using (either behaving the same way ourselves, or compensating against that behaviour), we are well on the way to changing it.

The next step in the healing process involves noticing how much we judge, attack and torture ourselves whenever we are acting or believe that we are acting in that certain way. This self-attack literally locks in the problem. To change it, we simply need to make another choice. We need to recognise that we have a choice between attacking ourselves, or helping whoever it is that we have caught in self-torture by projecting our own issues onto them. It is a simple choice: do we want to torture ourselves, or help them? If we decide to help them, we must leave the self-attack behind in order to do so. One of the main reasons why our ego sets up self-attack is to make us deaf to the calls for help around us. It is also to keep us closed to receiving or moving forward in our lives. Healing projection is a profound healing tool for transforming our world and the people around us. We let go of the self-attack long enough to extend ourselves out to support them. By no longer judging ourselves, we can both help others and transform our perception of what is around us.

Exercise

Exercise I
Ask yourself what key person keeps you from being more successful in relationships. This could be your present partner, an ex-partner, a parent, etc. Do the following exercise: Notice your projection. Realise that it is your projection and pull it back. Recognise your style of either 'I do it too', or compensation, or both. Make the choice 'Do I want to keep attacking myself or do I want to help them?' See yourself leaving your self-attack behind to help and support them.

Exercise II

You can also heal a projection through forgiveness, self-forgiveness or through integration. Integration occurs simply by choosing to melt the negative quality back into us. The negative quality disappears, although it remains available as an antidote for future negative situations. Its energy, which we have used as a negative self-concept, is melted back into us. Sometimes, if we have denied how strong this quality is, with the 'I would rather die than ever do something like that' type of compensation, it is helpful to integrate the projection with the compensation. In other words, integrate what we see them doing with how we act in an opposite way to hide it. Sometimes there are a number of self-concepts and compensations to integrate.

Exercise III

We can also use our intuition to go back to where the problem first began and heal it from there. It is much better to guess than to 'think' in these exercises.
Ask yourself:
'If I were to know when I judged this part of myself, if it occurred before, during or after my birth, it was probably:'

_____

_____

'If it was before my birth, at which month in the womb did it take place (from 1 to 9):'

_____

_____

'If it was after my birth, what year was it:'

_____

_____

'If anyone, who was present at this time:'

_____

_____

*'If I were to know what went on at this point that caused
me to judge myself and to bury this quality that I now
compensate for, it was probably:'*

_____

_____

*When you see, feel or sense the original scene, ask
your creative mind to return everyone present to their
centres, which is that place of peace or beingness, full of
grace and innocence. Sometimes the first time you ask is
enough and you are returned to a place of peace, bonding
and confidence. Sometimes you need to ask to go down
to deeper and deeper centres, until everyone in the scene
is at peace and reconnected once again. Peace, bonding
and centring occur naturally together. When one occurs,
the others naturally come about.*

WAY 46 Walking on the Shadow Side of the Street

All of us have shadow figures. Shadow figures are self-concepts that are not only negative, but also carry self-attack, self-hatred and give us the belief that we are bad, evil or nasty. While we typically might be aware of aspects of ourselves that we don't like, for the most part we bury the shadow figures we have. We forget them and then we forget we forgot them. We compensate for them by being good and nice, by working hard, sacrificing, or keeping difficulties in our lives, all to keep or pay off the guilt of the shadow figures hidden away. We use these compensations to prove that we are not really bad or evil, because we cannot stand the amount of self-hatred we have inside. Just as we have roles and behaviours to compensate for the shadow figures, and to prove that we are good, nice people, in the same way our shadow figures compensate for or hide our true goodness, power, love and the gifts that are inside us. The ultimate purpose for our shadow figures is to give us control over ourselves when we are frightened of our unlimited power, transcendence and greatness. Our shadows represent one of the best conspiracies we have against recognising ourselves as spiritual beings.

Out of fear of our powerful spiritual legacy and our

fear of God and our ego's fear that He would take over our lives, we create self-concepts about being bad or weak so we can hide in them. Because these evil self-concepts are so negative and destructive, we then create compensations for them. This is ultimately why bad things happen to good people. We are behaving like good people on the surface, but we have these negative self-concepts inside that are always begging for punishment. We are always attempting to pay off the guilt of the shadows within us by having upsets, setbacks or pain. This never works because the self-punishment of having scarcity (see page 223) or bad things happen to us only increases our bad feeling or guilt.

After years of working with shadow figures, I have found that where a shadow figure is recognised and integrated, we receive all of the energy back in a positive way. What had been negative now becomes an antidote or vaccination against future negativity in this regard and the internal conflict is ended. The ego uses shadow figures to keep us away from certain areas of our mind that have been fractured off and effectively lost. Since we are frightened of our shadow figures, we keep avoiding those places in our mind where they are cached away. The ego uses shadow figures to conceal doorways to parts of our mind that it wants us to keep lost. The ego is like an old man living in fewer and fewer rooms in his house. It wants us to shrink into smaller and smaller versions of ourselves, where it has more and more control. As we move into expansiveness and generosity, love and giving, the ego melts away.

The 'smaller' we think we are, the bigger our ego. So the ego gains control of our mind in the guise of helping us, shutting down the parts of ourselves that were painful and fearful. It hides gifts that were frightening or areas of our mind that we lacked the confidence to handle.

We all have shadow figures inside. To heal them and win back parts of our mind, we must first find them. One way to find them is to catch yourself when you act in such a way that self-loathing comes from your actions. This type of self-hatred is the sure sign of a shadow figure. Another way is to find where we are in sacrifice, or compensating. This shows a place where shadow figures are hidden underneath. An example of sacrifice would be working hard or being religious or virtuous to prove we are good. This does not build our confidence or give us the natural reward of being good. For example, we act super honest and over-react anytime anyone impugns our honesty. This is a sure sign of a shadow figure of dishonesty. Whenever a person acts very strongly in a positive way, but over-reacts when that behaviour is doubted, or they don't receive the natural reward that comes from that positive way, they are hiding shadow figures.

Another way of finding the shadow figures within us is to see the shadow figures that seem to follow us around and scare us. Whatever frightens or angers us in any major way as we look at our world points to shadow figures we have inside. These could be perverts, murderers, thieves, molesters, bullies, fools or invalids, or many more. Also, people in the news that upset us, or create major reactions in us, are sure signs that we have beliefs about ourselves being that way also and have hidden these beliefs away as shadow figures. It is important to realise that the area of the mind where we keep our shadow figures is typically repressed and well defended. Yet these self-concepts can ruin our lives by ensuring that we receive next to nothing. Where we have shadow figures we have locked-in guilt and self-hatred. We believe we do not deserve to have true love. We will feel unworthy of going to the next step in true love.

All personalities or self-concepts want to be in charge of our mind and run the show. From time to time, shadow figures may break out of the repression they are in and take over our conscious mind so that we actually act out some negativity that we later deny or that horrifies us. For instance, I have seen someone viciously attack someone else and then five minutes later have no memory of having done so. Sometimes we will have an alcoholic shadow figure that breaks out from where we have them imprisoned and goes on a binge. Another example is a person who is totally sane but occasionally an aspect of them emerges that acts really crazy. We have thousands of personalities. The shadow figures or negative personalities and self-concepts that we hate create conflicts with the parts of us that are moving in a positive direction. To transform ourselves and remove the invisible barriers in our lives that these shadow figures bring with them, we need to forgive ourselves for these shadows and reintegrate them. These parts of ourselves need to be loved, and when that occurs they will heal, mature, and naturally melt back into us as pure energy.

The hidden effect of shadow figures on relationships can be devastating. We may not allow ourselves to go into a relationship because we are afraid of the shadow within. If we have the belief that we are a destroyer, we will keep our present love at arms' length. I have seen people who had the shadow figure of the black widow. The black widow is the female spider that invites the male black widow over for lunch and they have a good time. Then the male black widow discovers he is the lunch. If this particular shadow figure is in a woman, she may keep her man at arms' length sexually because she's afraid she may actually kill him if they make love or get too close. Usually this occurs with people who are gifted sexually. Some people with this hidden shadow figure have spent years in loneliness, because they are afraid of harming someone they love. Some have even driven away their beloved for fear of harming them.

There are two more shadows that particularly affect our relationships. One is the demon woman, and the other is the hider. If a man has the demon woman, or the black widow, he will project them out on to his partner or on to women in general. The demon woman is the story of the demon that flies in at night through the open window, mounts the man and in this way, sucks all the bodily fluid out of him. In the morning, they find his body as a dried up corpse (sometimes with a smile). The effect of the demon woman is pretty much like the black widow shadow, but the demon woman is typically deeper, from an unconscious level. The hider, within either partner, is a hidden personality, withdrawn out of fear, guilt, or unworthiness. Where we have the hider, we do not give ourselves and nothing can be received. As a result we may have roles, but no authentic giving or receiving. This can rob us of love, fun, sex, or communication in a relationship leading to deadness, or it may be strong enough to keep us out of a relationship altogether.

Exercise

Examine the world around you for your shadow figures. Examine the people from the past who have been shadow figures for you. Write down what kinds of shadow figures they were for you. Take a look at the news around you. What kind of people upset you the most? Who brings up horror for you? What kind of shadow figures always seem to be peopling your world? Ask yourself how many shadow figures you have of each kind. Now take all of the shadow figures that you have discovered and melt them together until they are pure energy. Allow all that energy to come back into you and fill you once again. The negative beliefs that make up a shadow figure are mistakes. They are not the truth about you. They were the ego's way of blocking you from transcendence of your higher mind. Now it's time to unblock this way, clear the shadow figures that may have kept you from opening the door to true love and finding your beloved, or from going to the next step of turning your present partner into your beloved.

The ego is always quick to point out that we are negative or destructive. For instance, at times of lost bonding or trauma, at times of separation when we were children, the ego tells us that we stole our parent's gifts and killed them. This is then repressed and covered over with defence mechanisms such as pain and blame. That we are not thieves and murderers is easily recognised if we can bring these experiences to the surface and recognise them as an ego trap. Unless we realise and clear these and other common but deeply buried shadow figures, such as the failure, the orphan, the thief, the murderer and the betrayer, they will keep affecting and destroying our relationships. Our willingness to heal this and to know these negative beliefs are mistakes, allows us to go forward and build our life on a foundation of love. The shadow figures and the compensating sacrifice personalities can be integrated so we can move up to a whole new level of success.

Make a list of all of your shadows using the different ways of finding shadows. Include in it the legendary fairytale or historical characters you would most hate to be. This should give you a fairly big list. Now pick out the ones affecting your relationship or lack thereof. Now take the biggest shadow figure – the one you have discovered to be wreaking havoc in your relationship. Let us say it is the thief. Ask yourself how many thieves you have inside you. Imagine them all standing in front of you. Melt them all into one big thief. As you look at this thief standing in front of you, realise it is a hologram. Realise it is actually concealing a gateway to a deeper part of your mind. Now step into the shadow figure, right inside the hologram, and see the gateway there. Pass through the gateway and find the part of your mind that has been lost. Most of the time you will find a very positive area and as such it is naturally reclaimed. It will add more back to your mind than had been lost and closed off. This will give you more mind power and confidence.

Sometimes, we have closed off these lost areas of our mind because they are dark or fearful. If a new-found area of your mind seems negative, ask your higher mind to bring in the light to clear this part of your mind and free yourself. Ask for heaven's help so that dark area actually becomes a place of light, power, healing and help.

Healing the Fear of Loss

The fear of loss is one of the greatest traps into which we fall when we are trying to find true love or to become closer with our partner. All fear at some level is a fear of loss. When this occurs, people begin rewriting one of Shakespeare's famous lines, 'Better to have loved and lost than never to have loved at all' to read, 'Better never to have loved than to have loved and lost'. Many people tell me that the reason they are afraid of going into relationships or into a relationship with an extremely attractive partner is because they are afraid of losing them. Because they are afraid of never getting over that loss and not being able to go on in their lives, they choose not to love. Even within a relationship, we can have a fear of loss that freezes and paralyses us because we are afraid of not being able to handle the next step. As a result, we lose the relationship. We sometimes hide this fear of loss under a myriad of symptoms (particularly complaints) about our partner. We believe that they are the reason we are unable to go forward. Our partner's 'problem' is actually all about our fear of loss and losing control.

Now if you trace this back you would find a place in childhood where some bonding within the family was lost. As a result of this lost bonding, there began a feeling of loss and fear. So basically you have now come to a place in your relationship where you are re-facing that old fear and you are feeling that old loss as it is showing up now in the present relationship. Without awareness, most of us resort to some form of defence or control. Fear is right at the core of what is stopping us now in any of our problems and in that fear, there is a fear of loss. The loss and fear is then transferred to our present situation and we now have a chance to re-heal in our present relationship the loss that occurred when we were a child.

The original loss may also be passed down from generation to generation in our family and as such, it will be a strong and hidden pattern. This can show up as a fear or some other symptom that comes about as a result of fear. Usually when the problem is this big, there will even be a level of terror about moving forward. By moving forward or joining with our partner we have the ability actually to heal the whole pattern, or a layer of the pattern that has kept us stranded for such a long time.

Exercise

Examine your relationship or the lack of a relationship. Consider what the problem might be and what is missing. When this is accomplished, begin to look at your relationship situation as a situation brought on completely by your fear. Actually, it is brought on equally by everyone in the situation, but if one person transforms it, this will be shifted for everyone. *Identify your fear by imagining you are afraid of succeeding in relationships. What are you afraid would happen if you got a partner or if you went to the next step with your partner?*

Now imagine the person you love the most – child, parent, friend, spouse, lover – is standing across the room from you, with your fear putting a barrier between you. Any fear, like any grievance you have with anyone, will actually stand between you and everyone else. From across the room, see your potential partner standing next to the person you love most. What frightens you about moving forward to your potential partner? Share everything that comes to your mind. When you feel you can let that fear go, take a step toward them. One easy way to do this is to put it in the hands of God or your higher mind. As you go to the next step, imagine once again the person across from you. What scares you, or holds you back now? As you are ready to let this go, again, take a step forward to the next step.

Repeat this step-by-step, until you finally cross the room and imaginatively join them, holding them in your arms. This can repair the lost bonding by establishing it in the present. If you find any feeling of fear or symptoms of the problem coming up in the next week, repeat the exercise.

Over the years I have found that some people seem to have impossible parents or partners, or have gone through impossible relationship situations. Besides healing the element of projection, there is another important healing concept that has helped. It has to do with a person making a promise at a soul level to help another through an extreme problem, or to save them from themselves and their off-putting, negative behaviour. I have seen instances where this has been accomplished and the radically negative behaviour disappeared. I have seen other circumstances where layers and layers of healing needed to occur until the redemption was complete, but all the time, progress was being made and the chronic problem was improving. If we have had an extremely difficult person or situation in our life, we may have felt like the proverbial Job from the bible. If this is the case, we may already be resonating, or emotionally reacting, as we go through this particular chapter. If we had an 'impossible' person in our life, it will be easy to get everyone to agree that we are right. Because they were an 'impossible' person, it justified all our actions. If we left them, everyone would agree with us that we needed to get out of an abusive or impossible situation.

I am not counselling anyone to remain in sacrifice

or in an abusive situation, but I am suggesting that we may have other options before it gets to the point of abuse or leaving. We may want to complete the situation before we move on so it does not affect relationships to come. If we have moved on, we can complete it now in order to free ourselves of hidden guilt and unfinished business. It will also help our ex-partner. Our soul has set up this situation for a reason. At some deep level, what is going on around us with this problem person is only a reflection of the anger deep inside us. At this level where the other is a reflection of our mind, as we save them we save ourselves. At a soul level, it is more than likely that we may have made a promise to save this person. So no matter how much we feel justified in leaving, underneath there is still this feeling of guilt for not saving them. Even if the situation is long over, there is still something that can be done to help a troubled partner. Even if they have left their bodies, we can still remove that pattern or karma from their souls and ours and completely fulfil our promise.

Many people have chosen these impossible situations, or people, because of some life purpose. If they succeed in this trial or practice situation, if they give the gifts necessary to redeem a difficult person, there is no one they will not be able to save in a similar situation. I have seen this occur untold times. I have also seen that when someone did not complete this mission they were further plagued in their lives by unreasonable people in their work, family, acquaintances or friends.

The first thing that can help in such an extreme situation is the realisation of the principle that when someone is over-reacting, abusive, or acting in any negative fashion, they are in pain and need something. If we learn to supply the need we can be successful in situations where others are giving up. Of course, where we give help, we also receive help and we are open to receiving help in other situations where we are stuck.

The second principle is that of gift-giving. It is one of the things that has made the biggest difference in transforming problem situations in the past or present. I discovered this healing principle while working on the guilt that underlies our judgements, grievances and complaints. As I worked on this guilt, I found that the gift to remedy the situation was still intact underneath it. Let's say that a woman felt as if her father did not give her enough love and this had been her ongoing complaint in life. This led to a similar pattern with her partners. Underneath the complaint with her father, there were layers of guilt and feelings of failure that she had not saved her father. As I continued to explore this hidden layer of guilt, I found the gift of love and other gifts besides hidden beneath these layers. These were the gifts that she had come to give to her father to save him from himself. I found that as she gave this gift to her father, the guilt and feelings of not being loved dissolved. She now felt both loved and confident. She now had a gift to give to others. Once we have given our gift, we are finally open to receive a gift from the person to whom we have given.

The gift that comes in is one that seems to fill us deep inside. Usually, I will have a person close their eyes and imagine all of this taking place. It is especially helpful to do this at the point of where a pattern or a trauma began. Where there was conflict, there is now peace, confidence and a gift to respond to others in need.

Exercise

Practise filling the need with someone who is angry or complaining today. Whatever they seem to need, pour that into them. People who are complaining or angry are actually singularly open while they act out their feelings. If you imagine pouring love into them while they are carrying on, they tend to stop, or continue, but never quite in that same way again.

Go back to your relationship with your parents. What were your complaints? Go back to those situations imaginatively. What gifts to help them do you have inside under your complaints and your feelings of failure? See and feel yourself giving the gifts you brought for them. Enjoy the love, peace and feelings of completion. Now give to your parents any gifts you promised to give them as a couple. When that is complete, give the gifts you promised to give as a family. Now receive the gifts back from your parents, individually, from them as a couple and from the whole family. As layer after layer of issues come up with your family, this is one the easiest ways to move though it. Be aware of how your family changes. As the next layer surfaces, what gift do they need now? Look inside and you will find it. Share it and receive what they have for you now. Now go through all of your past significant relationships and complete the gift-giving and receiving with them.

WAY 49   The Ego's Strategy

As a regular surveyor of the subconscious mind and a spelunker of the unconscious or soul level, I know that our life is basically how we want it to be. This may sound preposterous to you, but over the two and half decades that I've been cruising the subconscious I have had some mind-blowing experiences. They demonstrated to me, time and again, that we choose what happens to us because we think it will make us happy. This has led to some terrible mistakes in our choices and our life. Here is a typical scenario that many people go through from just one dynamic of the subconscious. Our ego suggests we have a traumatic experience to try and pay off guilt. We then have the experience, but we also feel bad and guilty about the event itself. This sets up a vicious circle of guilt, victimisation to pay off the greater guilt, more guilt from the victim situation, etc. The ego tells us we have not merely made a mistake, but that we are wrong and guilty and we must be punished. Even when we consciously do not like what we have, we have chosen what is occurring from someplace within. Our ego's strategy will always fail us. It is time we consciously learned these strategies so we can make choices with awareness. When we follow the ego's strategies by allowing negative things to happen to us, it then blasts us with guilt and self-attack because of how bad we feel when we are victimised.

Guilt is just one of the destructive mistakes generated by the ego. There are others, such as grievances, holding on, revenge, victimisation as a form of attack, control, fighting and competition. What I have learned is that in spite of our mistaken strategies, we are all innocent. We all feel guilt but it is not the ultimate truth. Guilt keeps us caught in the same trap rather than allowing us to learn the lesson and to move on. On the other hand, we are responsible for our life and experience. Where we are responsible, we have power. The negative and traumatic events come about through mistaken choices that we immediately hide from ourselves. Here we feel victimised, unaccountable and weak.

These mistaken choices are the ego's strategy to help us, but they only partially work. They never work in the long term and they never make us happy. They just work to keep the ego in place. The longer we stay stuck, the stronger our ego. These events represent a strategy to get something, to protect ourselves, to pay off guilt, to defeat or attack others, to prove things to ourselves or others, to have an excuse, to hide from our purpose, to gain control of ourselves or others, to revenge ourselves, or to attempt to save our families. As we take responsibility for our lives and the many opportunities for healing that can make our lives better, we become more aware of what we have hidden from ourselves and we can make new, empowering choices.

In helping people through traumas or chronic

problems, the key is to love, support and connect
with the person that I am helping. When I have
reached and joined them, then we can begin to
explore effectively what was hidden and to make new
choices. So let me start by extending my support to
you, the 'you' who is reading this page. I can not see
you, but know I am here in my words, in between
the lines, wanting the best for you – wishing and
choosing true love for you and freedom from your
problems and pain. Now let me share some of what
I have learned to help people out of traps. Whether
you believe it or not, it can help. Whether you
accept the concepts or not, feel myself, my support
of you, wherever you are, whoever you are. Feel my
friendship as I extend it over these pages.

Exercise

*Now let's examine the situation. We think we want a
partner. We think we want to be as happy as possible in
our present relationship, but we don't have a partner, or
we have an unhappy situation with our present partner.
The principle that what we have in our lives reflects what
we want may go against what we consciously think we
want. To get beyond the propaganda of the conscious
mind, let us pretend this principle is true. We have what
we want. Whatever our situation is, let us pretend that it
is what we want. If we do not have a partner, or we have
a problem with our partner, let's pretend that is what
we want. Just for a moment imagine; I don't want a
partner . . . or . . . I don't want intimacy with my
present partner.*

Why?

_____

_____

How could you possibly want this?

_____

_____

What would having it this way allow you to do?

_____

_____

What would you not have to do by keeping things this way?

_____

_____

What are you trying to get by keeping things as they are now?

_____

_____

What fear are you trying to protect?

_____

_____

What guilt are you trying to pay off?

_____

_____

Who are you trying to defeat?

_____

What excuse does this give you?

Who are you getting revenge on?

What success are you afraid you cannot handle?

What inadequacy do you feel about succeeding at the next level?

Who are you trying to control and about what?

Who are you trying to dominate?

How does your present situation help you avoid your purpose in the world? Your relationship purpose?

What are you trying to prove?

_____
_____

What family roles are you playing that do not allow for your success?

_____
_____

What are you afraid you would lose?

_____
_____

Who are you holding onto from the past that does not allow you to move forward?

_____
_____

What are you holding onto from the past that does not allow you to move forward?

_____
_____

As you ask yourself these questions, there will be a stronger emotional response to some of them. Did these hidden attempts succeed? What would you like to choose now? If you're not sure, ask your higher mind to decide for you, or to show you the way to success in your relationships.

WAY 50 The Path of Relationships

The path of relationships is the quickest path of growth. Through the healing path of relationships, growth that would take hundreds of years of fighting temptations or decades of meditation can be accomplished in a much shorter time frame. Everything between you and your wholeness, the realisation of oneness, will come up in your relationship. Every bit of unfinished business with family members, old loves, friends, etc. *will come up disguised as problems in the here and now of relationships.*

Actually, this is the good news because it is these blocks inside us that stop us. So even though this old pain in new forms is uncomfortable to confront, if you face it with the right attitude it becomes a way to heal and move forward time and again. Once you commit yourself to your partner and love him or her more than your own story, your love can stop time and start eternity. The support of a loving relationship allows you to face the deepest layers of pain successfully and if you adopt the right attitude you will soon recognise the process is healing and helping you mature. And you will swiftly learn your partner is not your enemy. Once you give up your need to be special, you can have love and learn to be harmless in a way that provides true safety and allows a 'joining' which makes miracles possible.

Once you stop attacking your partner because of your or his or her needs, or blaming your partner for what you are doing (which is what we always do), then you have the possibility of leaping forward, sweeping blocks aside and finding solutions in a time-transcending way.

A relationship teaches you to receive, which is crucial to your own personal growth and to be a partner, which is crucial for your mental, emotional and spiritual growth. As you partner with your mate, you learn to partner with your higher mind and to allow the power of grace to come into your life, rather than having to 'do' everything yourself. 'Doing it' yourself locks you into a kind of independence which makes any relationship a fight or struggle. 'Doing it' yourself means it may or may not get done. But 'doing it' with the grace of the higher mind means it will be accomplished easily.

The truth is it is easy to find your perfect mate but much harder to keep him or her! Finding your perfect mate is the beginning of a great adventure in love and consciousness. Decide now that you are going to find – *and* keep – your perfect mate. Decide now that you will learn all the lessons you need to learn to keep the relationship unfolding gracefully. Decide now to become an expert on those things that support life and love: intimacy, communication, forgiveness, trust, giving and receiving, commitment and letting go.

Choose to commit with your partner to realise your wholeness rather than making your relationship the battleground of specialness and needs.

Choose now to develop a relationship with your higher mind, for that will naturally lead you into openness, partnership and living a life of grace.

Exercise

Focus on becoming an expert on the path of relationships so your love will create miracles.

Choose the path of relationships to accelerate your own healing and growth.

Intend that your perfect partner comes to you as part of your healing path or that you and your present partner break through time and again to new levels of love and romance.

The great adventure has just begun. May you choose to have smooth sailing. And may your story be a happy one!

I intend to find and keep my perfect mate in a loving and fulfilling life!

Glossary

Bonding The connection that exists between us and others. Bonding creates love and success with ease rather than with struggle and difficulty. It is what gives cohesiveness its glue and teamwork its mutuality.

Compensation Compensation is an attempt to make up for something negative by acting in an opposite way, in a role-like fashion.

Conspiracy A chronic trap of the ego, set up so well that it looks like we will never escape it. Conspiracies are particularly difficult to heal until we realise that the problem has been set up that way.

Ego The part of us that seeks separation and special-ness and – ultimately – wants to be God. It is the part of us that fights for itself and its own needs first. It is built on fear, guilt, negativity and competition, wanting to be the best of something, even if it is painful, or the best of the worst. Ego distracts, delays and attempts to stop evolution, being more concerned with its own continuity. It is based on domination-subjugation, rather than any form of strength or truth. It is ultimately an illusion. We make it strong, while we are young and then melt it away for partnership and grace.

Fusion A muddling of boundaries that occurs when bonding is lost. We cannot tell where we end and another begins. Fusion is the ego's answer to the lost intimacy. It is counterfeit bonding, which creates sacrifice and builds resentment. Fusion sets up an overburdening sense of loyalty. This eventually causes us to burn-out and move into the opposite extreme of independence. We move from over-caring and smothering to acting as if we do not care.

Gifts Aspects of greatness or grace that make any job easy. Our gifts are the answer to all situations because they remove the problem. Gifts are learned lessons that continuously give and create flow. They are packets of wisdom, healing and responsiveness for the situation at hand. In every problem, there is a potential gift. We have thousands of unopened gifts within us that are the antidote to pain and problems.

Higher Mind The aspect of the mind that is creative, contains or receives all of our answers, opens our will and our spirit to the grace that heaven and the world around us want to bestow on us. It is always guiding us with a quiet voice toward the truth. It encourages us to win together, not only now, but also in the future.

Love This is the ultimate goal and the best means to the goal. It is the sweet fulfilment that comes of an open-hearted extension of oneself. This is the giving, receiving, sharing and reaching out to one another. Love is the foundation of being and the best description of God, whatever your religious beliefs. It gives us everything we want – meaning, happiness, healing, nurturing and joy. Our evolution and happiness are based on how much we give and receive in love.

Manifest Consciously using the mind to choose what we want. It is the use of visualisation, feeling and sensing what we want and then letting it go and trusting. It allows us to create exactly what we want in detail.

Sacrifice A role that we take on to defend against a loss. When we are in sacrifice we give, but we do not receive, looking to lose now in the hope of winning later. Sacrifice is ineffective, blocking intimacy in an attempt to have the safety of a defence rather than equality and closeness.

Scarcity A fear-based belief that there is not enough and that we, or someone else, will have to go without. A belief in scarcity sets up power struggle, competition and sacrifice.

Shadow Figures Self-concepts that we have judged about ourselves and as a result, repressed. They represent areas of self-hatred that we project out onto others around us or onto the world in general.

The Stages of Relationships All relationships go through stages on their way to making heaven on earth. Each stage has its own challenges, traps and answers. If you know the stages of relationships, you are better prepared to handle the challenges and not to be blind-sided by the issues.

1. Relationships begin in the Romance or Honeymoon Stage, where we idealise the other, yet it is in this stage that we can see and feel the potential of the relationship.

2. Then there is the Power Struggle Stage where we are learning to bridge our differences, communicate, join and integrate both positions. Here we project our shadow figures on our partner and primarily fight for our needs.

3. The Dead Zone is a stage where we are learning to transcend good form for authenticity, find our worth without roles or sacrifice and learn how to bond, moving beyond the counterfeit bonding of fusion.

4. The Partnership Stage is where we have reached a balance between our own masculine-feminine sides and, correspondingly, we do so in our relationship, with our partner, finding balance, equality and intimacy.

5. The Leadership Stage is where we have both become leaders in life and have learned to value each other beyond the conflict and competition of personalities.

6. The Vision Stage occurs when we have become a visionary along with our partner, making contributions to the earth and healing unconscious pain and fractures.

7. The Mastery Stage of relationships is where we have healed our feelings of failure and valuelessness to the point of moving from doing and becoming, to being and grace. This is where we become living treasures to the earth. It is the beginning of heaven on earth for our relationship.

Further Information

About the Psychology of Vision

PSYCHOLOGY
VISION
of

For details on other books, the full range of audio and videotapes, and world-wide seminars, please contact us at:

Psychology of Vision UK
France Farm
Rushall
Pewsey
Wiltshire SN9 6DR
UK
Tel: +44 (0)1980 635199
e-mail: promotions@psychologyofvision.com
website: www.psychologyofvision.com

Also by Chuck Spezzano
(and available from the Psychology of Vision):
The Enlightenment Pack
Awaken the Gods